ZERO DEBT
The Ultimate Guide to
Financial Freedom

Third Edition

D1398882

Lynnette Khalfani-Cox

ADVANTAGE WORLD PRESS

Published by Advantage World Press
An imprint of TheMoneyCoach.net, LLC
P.O. Box 1307
Mountainside, NJ 07092

Book Packaging: Earl Cox & Associates Worldwide - http://earlcox.com
Cover Design: Marites D. Bautista

ISBN 10: 1-932450-70-X
ISBN 13: 978-1-932450-70-5
LCCN: 2016954288

Printed in the United States of America
Third Edition: 2017

SPECIAL SALES
Advantage World Press books are available at special bulk purchase discounts to use for sales promotions, premiums, or educational purposes. Special editions, including personalized covers, excerpts of existing books, and corporate imprints, can be created in large quantities for special needs. For more information, write to Advantage World Press, Special Markets, P.O. Box 1307, Mountainside, NJ 07092, or e-mail: info@askthemoneycoach.com

Publisher's Note

The information in this book is deemed accurate and correct. However, due to potential changes in the law and ongoing developments in the financial industry, readers are encouraged to verify the information provided.

Table of Contents

Other Books By Lynnette Khalfani-Cox, The Money Coach®

Zero Debt for College Grads: From Student Loans to Financial Freedom (Zero Debt Series)

College Secrets: How to Save Money, Cut College Costs and Graduate Debt Free

College Secrets for Teens: Money-Saving Ideas for the Pre-College Years

The Money Coach's Guide to Your First Million: 7 Smart Habits to Building the Wealth of Your Dreams

Your First Home: The Smart Way to Get It and Keep It

Investing Success: How to Conquer 30 Costly Mistakes & Multiply Your Wealth

The Millionaire Kids Club Volume #1: Garage Sale Riches

The Millionaire Kids Club Volume #2: Putting the 'Do' In Donate

The Millionaire Kids Club Volume #3: Home Sweet Home

The Millionaire Kids Club Volume #4: Penny Power

Acknowledgements

I can't believe *Zero Debt* is in its third edition, something that would never have been possible were it not for the love, personal support and professional guidance I've received from my dear husband and book agent, Earl Cox. Thank you, Earl, for teaching me nearly everything I know about successful book publishing – including how to make it to the New York Times bestsellers list. I'll never forget that it was you who first counseled me to write *Zero Debt* so many years ago. I'm so grateful that I listened to your wise advice. But I'm even more grateful that I married you. Earl, I am more in love with you today than I was on our wedding date and that – along with raising our kids – is what I count as my biggest success in life.

Speaking of kids, my three incredible children, Aziza, Jakada and Alexis, continue to inspire and motivate me. Thank you to each of you for the gift of motherhood and the joy you bring me.

Finally, a special word of thanks to Thomas Senkus: I am so deeply appreciative for all your help in editing and updating *Zero Debt*. You are so easy to work with and your assistance made this book a whole lot easier to complete.

Introduction

Would it be too much of a stretch to call debt the single biggest financial problem facing Americans today? I don't think so.

When I first wrote *Zero Debt*, I described credit card bills as the most heinous financial plague afflicting Americans. That was back in 2004. Since that time, the debt crisis in the United States has worsened dramatically – and now credit card bills aren't the only worry for U.S. consumers. A host of other debts are crippling people as well, including sky-high college debt, massive car loans and unaffordable mortgages too.

Although the Great Recession has officially ended, many people are still feeling the pinch of debt and recent statistics suggest Americans' debt woes are about to get even more severe:

- Credit card debt is climbing at a steady clip, on track to hit a record $1 trillion in 2017, data from the Federal Reserve show
- In the second quarter of 2016 alone, consumers racked up $34.4 billion in credit card debt, the largest second-quarter tally in 30 years, according to WalletHub's 2016 Credit Card Debt Study
- Student loan debt in the U.S. is at an unprecedented $1.3 trillion and rapidly growing each month
- Auto loan debt stands at $1.1 trillion, the highest levels to date

- Mortgage foreclosures dipped to a decade low in 2015, but 1.1 million homes in the U.S. still had foreclosure filings and mortgage debt totals nearly $8.5 trillion
- Nearly 1 million U.S. households filed for bankruptcy protection in 2015 because people couldn't pay their bills
- The national savings rate is the U.S. is in the flat-to-negative territory, similar to the Great Depression

America may be the "land of opportunity" and one of the riches countries on the planet. But that doesn't mean everyone is sharing in this country's wealth. In fact, there is cause for serious alarm for most of the nation's citizens. Despite the economic recovery, the numbers paint a clear picture of ongoing financial stress for far too many people.

But those are just statistics, and those figures may or may not be relevant for you or someone you know. So I want you to make things personal for a moment. Forget about stats and research. Just do a gut check and answer a few questions honestly.

- Do you ever worry or feel stressed out about your bills?
- Are you living paycheck to paycheck?
- Do you ever argue with your spouse or family members about money?
- Have you been forced to put off certain dreams – like buying a home, saving for retirement or launching a business – just because you can't afford to save for or fund these goals?
- Would you like to have more money in the bank each month, instead of turning over your hard-earned cash to creditors?
- Is it difficult for you to stick to a budget and juggle today's financial responsibilities, let alone set aside money for the future?

- Have you had to use credit or borrow money from a family member or friend in the past year or so to get by?
- Have you been asked to give or loan money to someone in need recently?

If you said yes to any of these questions, you likely have a glimpse of what it's like to struggle financially. And if any of these scenarios sound familiar, you're not alone. The sad truth is that the vast majority of Americans are living on the edge financially, with far too much debt and far too little savings.

Now don't get me wrong. Not *everyone* is carrying credit card balances – and I don't want to paint a picture of total financial doom and gloom, because that's definitely not the case. In fact, 35% of adults in the U.S. pay their credit cards in full each month. Unemployment – which had peaked at 10% in October 2009 – fell near the end of President Barack Obama's tenure, to just 4.9% in August 2016. Furthermore, some Americans have made real economic gains over the past decade. In September 2016, the Census Bureau revealed that median household income in the U.S. rose by 5.2% to $56,516 in 2015. That marked the first increase in median income since 2007, and it was the single biggest gain in income since the 1960s. Census data also showed that poverty in America dropped in 2015 to 13.5% from 14.8% in the prior year – the single largest decline in poverty in about five decades.

But none of that changes a host of other disturbing trends. For starters, among the two-thirds of Americans who do have revolving credit card bills, the average credit card debt is $15,310, according to NerdWallet. Additionally, two-thirds of Americans don't even have $1,000 saved to deal with an emergency, according to The Associated Press-NORC Center for Public Affairs Research. And we're not just talking about low-income folks here. That includes those making between $50,000 and $100,00 a year. Even worse: 66 million Americans have *no savings at all*, according to a Bankrate. com survey.

Some of you are just trying to make ends meet, charging basics like groceries, gas and medical bills. But others can't resist whipping out your Visa or MasterCard to satisfy your every whim, from designer handbags and fancy clothes to home furnishings and exotic vacations. I'm not here to pass judgment on what you choose to buy – especially because I've been guilty of poor spending choices too. But I am pointing out that no matter what you're purchasing, the result is destined to be the same: if you're constantly using credit cards to finance your lifestyle, you're setting yourself up for long-term economic failure.

It may not hit you this month, or even this year. But sooner or later, you're going to hit rock bottom. You may not even see it coming. Yet some unexpected setback will happen – like being laid off from your job, or going through a divorce – and all of a sudden, your debts will feel completely overwhelming. Think you have problems now? Well, that's nothing compared to what's in store if you allow your debt to continue spiraling out of control. That's when the fretting and sleepless nights really begin. Nasty debt collectors will start calling you at all hours of the day and night. Your credit rating will suffer due to missed payments. And you'll dread opening your mail because you can't stomach the thought of facing yet another bill. Unfortunately, ignoring the problem won't make it go away. Refusing to deal with your debts only causes you to keep living paycheck to paycheck.

Living the Bling Bling Life

Perhaps you're in that situation now. Those of you living what I call "the Bling Bling" lifestyle know exactly what I mean. Yes, you've got all the outward appearances of success – maybe a nice car, fine clothes, a closet full of shoes, various trinkets, gadgets and electronics galore. But none of these things are putting money in your pocket. None of these possessions build your net worth. In fact, deep down you know that despite all the material goods you've amassed over the years, your life is far from secure financially. You work hard, but have little of value to show for your efforts – and your debt is a big part of the problem.

Now you can stick your head in the sand if you want to, and pretend that everything is okay. Or you can face the truth about the debt problem in this country – and most important, your own debt problem – and you can begin to turn things around. The good news is that, believe it or not, you can make an incredible transformation in your personal finances in just 30 days.

I Went From $100,000 in Debt to Zero Debt & You Can Too!

Some of you may know that I'm a financial journalist by background and trade. You may have read my articles in the *Wall Street Journal, Essence* magazine, or online at AARP.org. Or, perhaps you watched me on television when I was a reporter for CNBC, or when I was a guest expert on CNN, *Oprah, Dr. Oz* or *Good Morning America.* What many of you may not have known, however, is that at one point I was *very deep* in debt – to the tune of *$100,000 worth of credit card bills alone.*

Fortunately, I managed to pay them all off – in less than three years –without ever missing a single payment. And no, I didn't file for bankruptcy protection to get rid of my debts. Nor did I cut up my credit cards and go into one of those debt settlement programs advertised so often on the radio or television. Instead, I got smart: about my spending, how I was handling my money, and especially how I was managing my credit and debt. I paid off every that dollar I owed and dug myself out of debt one step at a time.

After I became debt-free, I wrote *Zero Debt*, and it soon became a *New York Times* and a *Business Week* bestseller. *Zero Debt* is written as a 30-day action plan to help you wipe out debt, improve your credit, and jump start your finances – no matter what your current situation.

Zero Debt has touched a nerve with tens of thousands of readers, around the country and around the world, because debt is such a huge issue for so many people. And I mean *all* people: black and white, Asian and Latino; young and old; highly-educated and not; well-paid workers along with those making minimum wage.

All of the strategies I used to get out of debt – and more – are outlined in this book. I'm pleased to say that it's been 12 years since the original publication of *Zero Debt* in 2004, and here it is in 2016, and I still have zero credit card debt. I also have zero student loans and no car loan either. My only remaining debt is my mortgage, which my husband and I are on an accelerated payoff plan to eliminate as well.

Unfortunately, though, over the past decade or more, scores of other people have become mired in additional debt. More significantly, the entire credit and debt arena has changed dramatically. Here are a few highlights of some of the important developments that prompted the need for this revised, updated edition of *Zero Debt*:

- A sweeping overhaul of the bankruptcy system
- The rise of new credit scores, including VantageScore

- The rise of social media and related online identity theft
- Credit card reform legislation

As a result of these and other important changes, this revised version of *Zero Debt* not only provides fresh insights and updates throughout the book, it also contains 25% more content than the previous versions.

Shift from Over-Spending to a Debt-Free Life

When I give financial workshops or keynote addresses around the country, I often cite a study from Northwestern Mutual which found that more than 40% of Americans in all income categories spend an average of $1.22 for every dollar that they earn. That overspending explains, in part, why excessive debt is the number one financial problem in this country. But trust me: if I could rid myself of $100,000 in debt in just three years, you can get out of debt and achieve financial freedom, too.

My goal in revising and updating this book is to give you greater knowledge, skills and inspiration for living a debt-free life. Not only will I give you new pointers about how to achieve Zero Debt, I'll also offer you some unconventional personal finance advice, including some pearls of wisdom no one has probably ever shared with you. If you're sick of making those credit card payments month after month – and year after year – without really getting ahead, it's about time you learned the secrets of achieving Zero Debt. Otherwise, you're bound to continue in the financial rat race, spinning your wheels, working hard but aimlessly in a fruitless bid to rid yourself of credit card debt and other bills. Getting out of debt isn't rocket science, but it won't happen by accident, either. To eliminate your debt, you need a game plan.

Zero Debt is that plan. It's simple. It's easy to understand. And it works. Try it for yourself. With all the debt you're carrying around, what have you got to lose – besides that stack of bills piling up each day?

Two Groups of People Who Are Deep In Debt

As a Money Coach, I've learned that individuals who are deep in debt generally fall into two categories. The first group can be classified as "over- spenders and poor money managers." These are people who've never learned to manage their money the right way – simply because no one's ever taught them basic money-management skills. Others among them are just serious spenders. They've bought into this materialistic society that tempts us to always want more. That was my problem. When I was deep in debt I was a classic over-spender. I was actually earning a six-figure salary. But I was spending as if I earned seven figures. Trips to the Caribbean. Time shares. Expensive private school for my two older children. You name it. If I wanted it, I got it – mostly on credit.

Watch Out for the Dreaded Ds

The other set of consumers who are deep in debt have fallen victim to circumstances in their lives, misfortunes that I call the Dreaded Ds. This refers to anyone who has suffered a:

- Downsizing
- Divorce
- Death in the family of the main breadwinner
- Disease

- Disability
- Disaster (natural or man-made)

If any one of those things happens to you or somebody in your family, it can throw your finances out of whack and force you to live on credit.

Are You in The Debt Danger Zone?

It's possible that none of the Dreaded Ds has ever happened to you. But chances are you've experienced at least one of these setbacks – or you will in the future. However, you shouldn't have to go through a major personal or financial disaster before you take action to rein in your debt. If you're smart, and I know you are, you'll want to pay attention right now to the warning signs that you have too much debt. Unfortunately, a lot of us are in denial about whether we have a problem with debt and credit management. If you're making your credit card payments on time, if you have a decent job, or if you earn a reasonably high income, you might not realize you are in a "danger zone" in terms of your debts and bills. But don't be fooled. You have too much debt or are mismanaging your credit if you:

- are maxed out on any credit cards – or very close to your limits
- use credit card checks to pay for other credit card bills
- skip payments you can't afford
- don't even know how much debt you owe in total
- switch cards to get lower interest rates just so you can afford the minimum payments
- argue a lot with your partner or relatives about bills

Day 1: Stop the flood of credit card offers

Ever notice how your mailbox seems to be flooded with credit card offers every week? If your residence is like the average U.S. household, you probably get dozens of credit card solicitations in the mail each year. To put an end to them, simply call 888-5-OPT-OUT (1-888-567-8688) or go online to www.optoutprescreen.com.

The toll-free number I've given you, 888-5-OPT-OUT is an automatic phone service that's run by the four main credit reporting agencies: TransUnion, Experian, Equifax, and Innovis. (Many of you may be thinking: *"What is Innovis?"* I'll tell you more about that company – and the credit report you've probably never even heard of – later, in **Day 4**. For now, though, let's stay with this OPT-OUT number).

The reason this number works is because it takes you out of the credit bureaus' databases for pre-screened mailings. This will force the credit bureaus to stop selling your name and address to banks and other institutions that send you credit card offers each month.

Research companies and public-interest groups, such as the Consumer Federation of America in Washington D.C., track the rate at which banks and other credit card issuers send out credit card offers. They've discovered that roughly four to six billion credit card solicitations are sent to people like you and me every year. Imagine: a whopping six *billion* credit card offers, or roughly 60 per U.S. household! According to the Mail Monitor report from Synovate, a Chicago research firm, 90% of credit card mail comes from the 10 largest credit card issuers. Furthermore, even though smart phone and Internet use are commonplace, and 97% of credit card applications are made online, banks still rely heavily on good old-fashioned snail mail. According to Mintel Comperemedia, credit card direct mail offers grew by 16.12% to 1.52 billion mailings in the first quarter of 2016 compared to the first quarter of 2015. American Express, Capital One, Chase, Citibank and Discover represented the top five credit card solicitors.

If you're wondering why in the world banks send out so many darned solicitations, the obvious answer is because they're hunting for new clients. But the less obvious reason is that financial institutions are also responding to changing customer demand. When interest rates rise, banks often increase their mailings because with higher interest rates, people often start looking for fixed rates products on things like credit cards and mortgages. As a result, consumers are more likely to be receptive to new offers for credit. Still, if you're like most people, you probably tend to give credit card offers the cold shoulder – perhaps tossing them in the trash can without even opening them. That's why the average response rate to credit card solicitations is miniscule – just 0.6% according to the latest figures from the Direct Marketing Association. For all the mail being sent out, direct mail doesn't seem to be the most profitable way for credit card companies to do business. For starters, they have to send out more than 250 solicitations just to acquire one new customer. That means up to $200 spent to attract every new cardholder. And have no doubt about it: banks and other companies are marketing credit cards right now so aggressively that Americans are poised to have record levels of plastic in their wallets.

In 2008, the number of credit cards in America peaked at more than 496 million cards. But card volume dropped by nearly 25% amid the Great Recession and by late 2010, there were just 379 million cards in use -- manly because banks cut people off and closed accounts. Since then, however, credit card offers and credit card use have been steadily rising. In late 2016, there were roughly 450 million credit cards in Americans' wallets. By 2018, if current trends continue, the amount of credit cards in the U.S. is once again expected to reach record levels, perhaps exceeding 500 million credit cards. Needless to say, with more credit cards comes the prospect of more credit card debt for Americans.

Five Reasons to Opt Out of Credit Card Offers

No matter how many tantalizing credit offers banks dream up, it's worth opting out of these pre-approved offers, for many reasons – especially if you're struggling to get rid of excessive debts.

1. For starters, you'll keep yourself from going deeper into debt by limiting the number of credit cards you have.
2. Additionally, you'll protect your credit score, because every time you apply for a new credit card, an "inquiry" goes on your credit file.
3. Reducing the number of credit card solicitations you receive can reduce your risk of being victimized by identity theft.
4. By opting out, you will also save yourself the time and effort of having to deal with so much junk mail day in and day out.
5. And last, you'll put an end to being frustrated by credit card companies that ultimately decline your application or turn you down for the amount of credit they originally used to tempt you.

For example, have you ever received a credit card offer in the mail, promising you "up to $20,000?" Then when you finally take the bait, and go ahead and apply for the blasted card, you wind up getting approved all right – but the limit is more like $2,500 or $5,000. If you ask why you didn't get the $20,000 limit or whatever was originally indicated on the credit card offer, the bank's reply will always be the same: "*Our decision was based on your credit history and current credit use.*" Sure it was. But they had a sense of your credit history when they first solicited you. You fit a certain profile, and that's why they made you the offer in the first place. So who needs that kind of tease – only to be disappointed? Do yourself a favor, and instead of getting frustrated with this system, opt out instead.

One Easy Phone Call Can Help

When you're ready to opt out of getting pre-screened offers and take your name off the credit bureaus' marketing lists, simply follow these instructions:

<u>**Step 1:**</u> Call 1-888-5-OPT-OUT (888-567-8688)
<u>**Step 2:**</u> Select *Option 1* if you want to opt out for five years (You can also choose to opt out permanently if you'd like).
<u>**Step 3:**</u> Follow the directions to enter your social security number, correct telephone number, address and name.

The recording will tell you that the information you enter is confidential and will only be used to remove your name from the list. After you're done providing your personal information, you will get a message from this service advising you that your request will be handled within five business days. If you have other people in your household who want to opt out, the 888-5-OPT-OUT service also gives you the option to leave information for an additional family member.

Once you opt out, be aware that you may still get some credit card offers in the mail. How so? For starters, it can take up to 60 days for solicitations to stop. But the main problem is this: Offers may come from any credit-granting companies that do not use these credit card companies to secure their list of pre-screened consumers. That's a frustration for many consumers – including my own husband. He's opted out in the past. And I recently opted us both out. But he still gets various solicitations, so this system definitely isn't ironclad. For now, however, it's what we have.

Opting Out Using the Internet

If you'd rather handle this process electronically, you have two opt-out options at http://www.optoutprescreen.com. Through this website, you can:

- Opt out from receiving credit offers for five years
- Opt out from receiving credit offers permanently (You can also get a "Permanent Opt-Out Election" form from this website that you mail in)

When you opt out electronically, you'll have to provide personal information including:

- Your Name
- Address
- Social Security Number
- Date of Birth

If you visit this http://www.optoutprescreen.com website, you'll find that the credit bureaus make it clear that you have the right to opt out. After all, they're required to tell you this by law. But you'll also find that they not- so-subtly suggest that you *not* opt out.

The way they do this, essentially, is by suggesting you that you'll miss out on offers for credit and insurance that could be financially prudent. They also suggest that keeping your name on the list for pre-approved credit offers is a way for you to get "first dibs," so to speak, on credit card offers before other people do. I don't buy either of these self-serving arguments. And if you're struggling with debt, neither should you.

What if You Change Your Mind?

Still, some people worry about opting out permanently, particularly if they think they might change their mind later, and actually want to get some credit card offers in the mail. For example: about two-thirds of all direct mail credit card offers include a rewards program – offering you perks such as cash back, points, miles and rebates. So once you get your debts under control, you might (wisely) want to take advantage of certain credit card benefits. If this is a concern for you, set your mind at ease. The credit card industry is far too smart to create an opt-out system that would be irreversible for consumers. So if you opt out, and you have a change of heart later, it's a very easy process to opt back in. Let's say you went online and previously completed an opt-out request electronically. Well, you can later reverse that decision and choose to *Opt-In* and once again become eligible to receive pre-screened credit card offers. A few other things: opting out does not hurt your credit score, nor does it affect your ability to apply for or receive credit or insurance when you want to apply for them.

Opting Out By Mail

If you don't want to use the phone or the Internet, you can also write to each one of the credit bureaus and request that your name be removed from their pre-screened lists. In your letter, state clearly that you want to "opt out" of credit card offers. Be sure to provide the credit agency with your name, mailing address, city, zip code and social security number. If you've moved within the past six months, don't forget to also include your old address. Regardless of whether you opt out, make sure you shred any pre-approved credit card offers before trashing them. This will help prevent crooks from getting credit in your name.

The Limitations to Opting Out of Credit Card Offers

When you opt out of credit card offers, it will greatly reduce the number of credit and insurance solicitations you get in the mail, but unfortunately, it won't put an end to all pre-approved credit offers. You'll still be subjected to pitches from local merchants in your area, religious groups, and all manner of charitable associations. Additionally, professional organizations, alumni associations, politicians, and companies with which you currently conduct business can all still legally solicit you. If you want to cut down on mail from these sources, or from any institution that may constantly send you generic mail with the title "Occupant" or "Resident," you have to write each one of these groups individually and specifically ask to have your name removed from their lists.

Put an End to Most Junk Mail

While you're at it, if you really want to stem the tide of junk mail you're getting – not just credit cards, but all solicitations. You may want to consider writing to the Direct Marketing Association. Tell this group that you'd like to add your name to their Mail Preference

Service. When you register for this service, your name and address are placed on a "do not mail" list. All DMA members must check their list of potential customers against the "do not mail" file. So if your name is on that list, the marketing company must remove you from its mailings. To get registered as soon as possible, you'll have to pay $1 and register online. In return, you'll get about 95% less junk mail for five years. You can also get on the Mail Preference Service list through the mail, by writing The Direct Marketing Association. This is a slower process, but it works.

The Direct Marketing Association reports that its "do not mail" file is updated each month and distributed four times a year: in January, April, July and October. The organization says you usually see a drop in the amount of mail you receive about one to three months after registering for their service. Again, it's faster if you use their online registration process. Also, if you move, you have to register your new address with the Mail Preference Service to make sure marketers don't start sending you unwanted mail again.

Here's how to reach The Direct Marketing Association:

Mail Preference Service
Direct Marketing Association
P.O. Box 282 Carmel, NY 10512
http://www.the-dma.org

Remember: not all companies use the DMA Mail Preference Service to purge their mailing lists. So, it's possible (likely, in fact) that you will still get some companies' promotions. When this happens, just contact the company directly and request that your name and address be placed on the company's "do not mail" list.

A Sweeter Offer?

I recall very clearly a time when I was up to my eyeballs in debt, but had just paid off one credit card in full. Suddenly, a barrage of new credit card offers appeared in my mailbox. One of them was a card with a pre- approved $20,000 credit line. Was it tempting? Only for about two seconds. I declined the offer. But I saved the form to remind myself that credit card issuers were never going to stop tempting me. It was up to me – and me alone – to exercise restraint if I wanted to pay down my debt, and properly manage my credit. You have to get your mind right. As persistent and aggressive as they are, why should credit card companies shoulder the *entire* blame for you accepting credit offers you shouldn't, and consequently overspending?

The Truth about Credit Card Companies

In fairness, I have to say two things in defense of the credit card companies:

First of all, believe it or not, they really don't want you to become so indebted that you can't pay your bills. I know that a lot of you mistakenly think that credit card companies love it when you're behind on your payments because then they can jack up the interest rate. After all, they're in business to make money. And one way they do that is by collecting interest charges on purchases. But creditors are also aware of the possibility that if things get really bad for you, you have the option to file for bankruptcy protection, which could give you the right to wipe out your credit card debt entirely. So trust me, they really don't want you to sink into a financial hole.

Are You Playing the Blame Game?

Second, every consumer has to take some level of personal accountability for his or her actions. The truth of the matter is that even with all the billions of credit card offers being extended each year, no one is putting a gun to your head and making you say "Yes."

Are all those offers tempting? Sure they are. But the credit card company alone can't be held solely responsible for your decision to say "Yes," any more than the restaurant waitress who comes after dinner with a cart full of delicious cakes, mouth-watering pies, and tantalizing chocolates, and asks: "Dessert anyone?"

Is she to be blamed for your ever-expanding waistline if you say "Yes" to dessert every time you patronize that restaurant? Of course not. Well, by the same token, it is not entirely the credit card company's fault if you choose to "bite" at their credit card offers and then find yourself in financial trouble.

What's the solution? If you don't have the restraint right now to say "No," and you haven't yet learned to properly manage your credit or spending, do yourself a favor and opt out of most credit card offers by calling 888-5-OPT-OUT or logging onto www.optoutprescreen. com. Do it right now. You just don't need that temptation.

The Low-Down on Credit Card Solicitations via Email

Some of you may have no problem tearing up those credit card applications or saying "*thanks, but no thanks*" to the telemarketers who call you to offer new credit.

But are you lured by those email offers for credit cards? In this age of the Internet and high-tech fraud, you need to be especially careful with these unwanted solicitations. If you get an email that supposedly comes from a bank where you're already doing business, but the sender of the email asks for your account number or requests that you "confirm" certain personal information, such as your address or social security number, please don't fall for this scam. Someone could be trying to steal your identity for their own financial gain. (Read more about identity theft and how to avoid it, in **Day 11**). Use common sense here. If a financial institution has an existing business relationship with you, they should already know your address and account number. So, asking you for it via email is ridiculous! Don't worry if the email says "*your account will be terminated*" if you don't reply by a certain date. More often than not, that's a big red flag that you *shouldn't* respond. Even if the email turns out to be legitimate, your bank or financial institution maintains records electronically. In the worst case scenario, if your account does get "terminated," – which I've never once heard of happening to someone under these circumstances – your bank will still have your account number and identifying information. So any account that mistakenly gets closed can easily be reopened.

Day 2: Make a resolution to "stop digging."

Famed billionaire investor Warren Buffett once said that if you find yourself in a hole, the first thing you must do is to "stop digging." It may sound basic, but every day, people with massive amounts of consumer debt continue to dig themselves deeper into the red by spending as if there's no tomorrow. If you *know* you've been over-spending, you must vow to end negative spending habits. This is *crucial* to fixing your finances. Let me put it another way: if you're serious about chucking your credit card debt, you have to put an end to frivolous or excessive spending – starting today!

So many of us tend to make empty promises to ourselves and others: promises that we'll spend less and save more; promises that next year we'll get our act together; promises that with the next promotion or the next bonus or the next money that comes in we'll make good use of that cash – anything related to whipping our finances into shape. It especially happens at the beginning of the year. Have you ever made a New Year's resolution concerning your finances? More to the point, if you have such a resolution going forward, chances are you'll need all the help you can get to stay on track. The December holiday season is the time of year that many of us tend to overspend – leaving us with big credit card bills and the equivalent of a shopper's hangover that lasts well into the following year.

For those of you determined to better manage your money, you don't have to live a life of deprivation in order to get into the black. The best way to turn your financial resolutions into lasting changes is to take some concrete steps that won't cramp your style, but will definitely improve your personal finances.

Here are some ways you can do just that:

- **Create a realistic financial plan**

  A proper financial plan provides you with a snapshot of where you are today – in terms of assets and liabilities, and your current cash flow. It also outlines your short-, medium- and long-term goals, such as saving for a down payment on a house or taking a dream vacation. Finally, a well- crafted financial plan should include a number of "must do" items, such as you must start contributing to your IRA or you must pay off your Visa bill.

  Don't make the mistake of thinking *"If only I could stay out of the mall, I could get my finances under control."* Staying out of the mall may be necessary for you die-hard shoppers who need to change your surroundings and avoid too much temptation. But getting your finances in order is not necessarily, and certainly not exclusively, about will power. It's about creating such an awesome plan of action that you don't want to deviate from it because you can clearly see all the benefits of having a financially sound household. After all, which of the following circumstances is most appealing? Scenario #1, in which you and your spouse are always bickering about money and you have to live paycheck to paycheck, or Scenario #2, in which you've lived within your means, and your money squabbles all but disappear? When you need motivation, remember that by sticking to your resolutions, especially your newly-created financial plan, you'll not only save yourself big bucks, you'll ultimately have financial freedom, and far less worries and stress about money.

- **Make this money resolution:**

"Before I buy something, I will think about *why* I'm spending. I will spend money only for the *right* reasons."

Why We Spend

We all dole out cash for things we need, such as food, clothing and shelter. But we also buy plenty of things just because we want them or because we feel: "I deserve it." After all, we all work hard for our money. So what's the big deal about splurging every once in a while, right? Well, the big deal is that if you're serious about getting out of a financial pit, your splurging days are over – at least for now.

You must also be careful of spending solely to impress others, like buying luxury cars or fancy jewelry just for show. Think about that for a minute. How many people do you know really just spend to show off the latest, the so-called best, or the most fashionable this or that? What good is having a Lexus or a Mercedes if you're still renting and don't own your own home? And whom are you really kidding if you're buying Gucci and Prada, yet you still worry about your credit card getting declined?

Other times, people spend simply because they're angry, depressed or bored. Maybe you just had an argument with your man – and ladies you know if I'm talking to you – and because he ticked you off, all of a sudden you're in the mall. Or perhaps a boss is frustrating you on the job, or a co-worker is getting on your nerves. So what do you do? You start spending as a temporary, quick fix *to feel better*. Try your best to avoid "retail therapy." That's when you start purchasing cosmetics or an expensive new pair of shoes (even though you have tons of each at home) in an effort to give yourself an emotional pick-me-up.

Make a point to avoid spending *out of habit*, too. Many of us literally spend money on habits – things like cigarettes or alcohol. If you've got such a habit, realize that it could be costing you your fiscal and physical health. Even those habitual patterns that aren't detrimental to our bodies might still be harmful to our bank accounts. For instance, I know many women who go to the hair salon, or get regular manicures and pedicures, mainly out of habit. They've always done it, it's routine to them, and practically nothing on God's green earth is going to stop them from hitting the salons week after week after week.

Now don't get me wrong. I like to look as nice and as put together as the next woman. But my point is that if you're struggling to pay your bills, can you really afford to fork over $50 a week (or whatever you might be paying) for the luxury of "beautifying" yourself? Personally, I don't think it's really worth it to look the part of "the fabulous diva" on the outside, when on the inside you're stressed out and feeling more like "the fake debtor" because everybody thinks you've got it all together, but deep down, you know the scary truth about your situation.

There's one other point about this subject that is worth addressing, in case you're thinking: *"Honey, getting my hair and nails done, that's not a **luxury**; it's a **necessity**!"* I'd like you to at least consider another perspective about certain things that we spend money on. Read the advice contained in **Day 16** for some insights about the ways we surrender our money on things that we might think are "necessities," but others consider "luxuries," "frivolous," or "downright wasteful."

By now some of you may be thinking: *Darn! Is there anything I can spend on?* And the answer is: Of course there is. Obviously you should feel free to spend money on the things you need. No one is suggesting that you walk around unclothed, without proper shelter or hungry. People will often say, "*Lynnette, I also need a car – I have to get to work.*" To which I answer, "*Yes, you **need** a car, but does it really have to be a **brand-new** one or a $50,000 vehicle?*" Just live within your means and be reasonable in your spending – even when buying the things you need.

You can, and also should, spend *to help* others — i.e. to aid your family, church or a favorite charity — when you can afford to do so. And it's even okay to open your wallet to buy, have or do what you *want* (think art lessons, graduate school or travel) in order *to improve* your quality of life, express your values, or invest in yourself or family members.

But I've discovered that a lot of us spend for the wrong reasons. Sometimes people spend to exert power and control over others: as when parents tell their high school or college-age children: "*I'll buy you XYZ, but only if you do what I say, or go to the school I choose,*" etc. Men (and women) have also been known to use money as a way to keep their significant others in check; or they buy them gifts in a misguided effort to secure the other party's love and affection – or even to get out of the doghouse after an argument or some exhibition of "bad" behavior. All of this crazy spending must cease immediately.

Wage War on Your Debt

You've heard of "Cease Fire" agreements when nations are at war, right? Well, right now consider yourself at war with your debt. It's a battle you'll win if you start off with a "take no prisoners" attitude. And that means beginning with the mindset that NO MATTER WHAT you will not spend beyond your means, you will not spend for the wrong reasons, and you will no longer pile on additional credit card debt. Instead of a "Cease Fire" agreement, you're now going to create a "Cease Spending" pact with yourself.

- **Write out your very own *"Declaration to Achieve Zero Debt."*** Use the following model as your guide.

I, insert your name here, *realize that I am in a financial hole. Therefore, I hereby vow to stop digging myself further into debt. I acknowledge that I can never be free from money worries if I continue to spend excessively, for the wrong reasons, or on unnecessary things. From this day forward (*insert month date and year*) I will be more conscious of my spending habits, being careful to keep my behavior in line with my desire to reduce my debt and achieve financial freedom.*

Get this statement free at my website, AskTheMoneyCoach.com. Print it and insert your name and date. Then put it in a visible place, as a reminder of your commitment to financially empower yourself.

Diagnosis: You're Suffering from the Debt Disease

Some of you who are over-spending have a real problem. In fact, you have a sickness, of sorts. Now before you think that I'm offering you a clinical diagnosis, let me say that I'm talking about a personal belief I have about people with massive credit card debt due to over-spending. I feel strongly that excessive debt is the worst possible financial cancer you can have. In fact, I believe that debt for many people is a byproduct of a terrible disease – an insidious malady known as *consumerism* – and as a symptom of a disease, debt should be treated as such.

If you think about it, many aspects of chronic spending, and the debt that results from it, are really no different from alcoholism. Check out the following 10 similarities:

Excessive consumerism and alcoholism both:

1. Generate stress and physical illness (migraines, ulcers, etc. can result from money worries)
2. Tear families apart (70% of all couples that divorce say financial strife was a major problem in their marriage)
3. Produce short-term euphoria or escapism from daily problems
4. Can be generational (Don't you know people whose behavior just mimics what their mom or dad did?)
5. Make individuals feel shame, guilt and embarrassment
6. Have complex underlying or root causes for their behavior
7. Cause victims to feel out of control with their actions
8. Produce hangovers (for the alcoholic, a drinking binge leads to a physical hangover; for the shopaholic, a spending binge creates a debt hangover that lasts months or years)
9. May require individuals to change their habits, their friends, the places they frequent, etc. to reduce temptations
10. Have similar and predictable phases of deterioration

– Denial

The phase where the person refuses to admit he/she has a problem, as in: *"I don't have too much debt," "I don't shop too much"* or perhaps: *"I can handle my bills."*

– Worsening of the problem

When the debts mount, late fees occur, bill collectors call, etc.

– Hitting 'rock bottom'

Characterized by traumatic financial events, such as foreclosure, bankruptcy, personal or business lawsuits, and so forth.

– Intervention

Sometimes the intervention is from within the family, as when a husband takes away his wife's credit cards. Other times, the intervention/help comes from an external source, such as when a person voluntarily goes to a debt management program.

Now that you can see the common areas between excessive consumerism and alcoholism, is it any wonder that debt has such a stranglehold on you?

But don't despair. You don't have to remain drunk with debt. You can kick your spending addiction, if that is what has put you in this mess. Each of you can break the cycle of debt. With the right know-how and some positive action, you truly can fix your finances, once and for all.

Again, it won't be easy. But I'm going to ask you to exercise a little faith – and a lot of *follow through*. In other words, please don't just *read* this book. Throughout the next 30 days, put my recommendations into practice, and you'll see your finances drastically improve.

Day 3: Put all your debts in writing

Today you're going to write down everything you owe your creditors. That's right, *everything* – from your student loans, to mortgages, to credit card debt, medical bills, auto loans, etc.

On a piece of paper, make a complete list of your obligations and here's what you should write or type out on the sheet: Include the name and phone number of each creditor, your account number, the interest rate you pay, the total balance due, and the minimum monthly payment.

Why Torture Yourself Listing All Your Bills?

You need this information in black and white to get a realistic picture of where you are. This info will also help you later when it's time to negotiate with creditors or collection agencies. Again, write down *everything* that you owe, even credit cards that might have only $100 on them. Don't make the mistake of leaving those "small" bills out because *"Oh, I'm going to pay that one off this month anyway."* Just write down everything you actually owe, as of today.

Many people have a rough idea about how much they owe their creditors. But there's no substitute for having true, accurate numbers – not guesstimates. To fill in the proper figures on your written sheet, or your computer spreadsheet, you'll have to go find your most recent statements and invoices from your creditors. Take as much time as you need today to collect all this data. It's a crucial step in you getting your finances together.

It's also a good idea to call the companies you owe and ask for the latest information about your debt, especially if you're looking at statements that are more than a month old. Even if the statements are current, you should call your creditors because some of the information on those statements may have changed. For instance, you may have charged additional items since the closing date on your credit card statement, so now your debt is actually greater than your current statement indicates. Also, you may have had a teaser rate or a lower interest rate in the past, and maybe that interest rate has now jumped. Whatever the case, you need to have the most accurate information that is currently available.

A Wake-Up Call: How Much Do You Owe?

The next step is for you to add up all your debts. For some of you, seeing your total debt in black and white may be a scary thing: a wake-up call to how deeply you are in financial bondage. For others, seeing your total debt may offer relief: perhaps you don't owe as much as you feared.

Whatever the situation, don't panic. Remember, you're on the path to financial freedom now and if your goal is to get to "Zero Debt" status, keep plugging along – it will happen, and sooner than you think!

I Debticate Myself to Being Debt-Free

If you need a little help to get your list of creditors down on paper, use this handy form on the next page that I've created, called "I Debticate Myself to Being Debt-Free." It's meant to give you an honest, black-and-white look at where you are today. Later, the form will also serve as an incentive when you're slashing your debts, one at a time. You can download a copy of this form from

I Debticate Myself To Being Debt-Free

Creditor	Account Number	Phone Number	Interest Rate	Balance Due	Minimum Monthly Payment
1.					
2.					
3.					
4.					
5.					
6.					
7.					
8.					
9.					
10.					
11.					
12.					
13.					
14.					
15.					

AskTheMoneyCoach.com

AskTheMoneyCoach.com, and then fill it in appropriately. You'll find this document under the "Free Info" area. Just click on the PDF that says "I Debticate Myself to Being Debt Free." Don't skip this step – do it today! At the very least, answer this question now: How many credit cards are in your wallet? A wallet full of plastic, especially charge cards that are at their limit, is definitely a warning sign that you're carrying far too much credit card debt.

DAY 4: Order your FICO® score

Keeping tabs on your credit score is always a smart idea. As I'll later explain, there are various credit scores. But the best-known one in the marketplace right now is the FICO score. You can certainly visit www.myfico.com to get your FICO® credit scores and your credit reports instantly online – but it'll cost you. At last check, the cost of obtaining three credit reports (your Equifax, Experian, and Trans Union reports) and your three FICO® credit scores at www.myfico. com was $59.85.

I do recommend getting all three reports, as sometimes one agency's credit report may list certain accounts or information about you that is not contained in the other credit bureaus' reports. And you obviously want the most comprehensive information contained in your credit files. Thanks to the FACT Act, you're also entitled to obtain your credit reports free of charge by logging onto www.annualcreditreport.com. At this website you'll also find your credit files from the "Big Three" credit bureaus –TransUnion, Equifax, and Experian.

The "Big Three" Credit Bureaus

You are entitled to receive one free credit report every 12 months from each of the national consumer credit reporting companies: TransUnion, Equifax and Experian. Some people like to order one report, wait six months, then order another credit report from a different bureau, then wait another six months, and order a third report form the last credit reporting company. This way, they can monitor their credit report throughout the year – free of charge. The downside to this approach, however, is that you never see all your credit reports simultaneously to get one complete snapshot in time of your credit files. This is important because different credit bureaus often have varying information. You want the information in all three credit files to be as accurate, complete and consistent as possible. And the best way to do that is to see all three reports at the same time. So I suggest that when you get your credit reports, request all three free reports at the same time, and compare them side by side. With each credit bureau, after you get your free report, you can't get another free one from that bureau for 12 months. If you want to see your credit file again before one year's time, you'll have to pay for the report.

There are a few other ways, though, that you can get free credit reports. If you ever get turned down for credit, you are automatically entitled to a free credit report under the Equal Credit Opportunity Act. Just make your request to the credit bureaus within 60 days of being denied credit. Additionally, if you are unemployed, very poor (or considered "indigent"), or have been the victim of identity theft, you are legally entitled to a free credit report under federal law. These credit agencies also offer a credit score, known as the VantageScore, which I'll address later in this chapter. For now, however, let me explain everything you need to know about FICO® scores. Then I'll explain VantageScores – as well as how you can get both FICO scores and VantageScores completely free of charge.

What is a FICO® Score?

For those of you who are unfamiliar with credit scores, you should know that practically all lenders use credit scores. Some 90% of all mortgages lenders use FICO® scores and 98% of the top 50 credit card companies use FICO® scores to determine whether or not to grant consumers loans, making FICO® scores the most popularly used credit scores in the country. FICO® stands for Fair Isaac Corporation. That's the Minneapolis-based firm that developed the credit scoring software used to assess your credit- worthiness. In short, banks and other financial institutions look at your credit score to determine whether or not to extend to you a mortgage, an auto loan, credit cards, and so forth. FICO® scores range from 300 to 850. The higher your score, the less a credit risk you are deemed. Translation: the higher your score, the more likely it is statistically that you will pay your debts on time. Therefore, those with better scores save money because banks will make lower interest loans to those consumers than they will to others with less-than-stellar credit records.

For instance, look at the difference in borrowing costs for anyone getting a $300,000 fixed rate, 30-year mortgage:

FICO® Score	Your Interest Rate	Your Monthly Payment
760-850	3.088%	$1,279
700-759	3.310%	$1,316
660-699	3.487%	$1,345
620-659	3.701%	$1,381
580-619	4.131%	$1,455
500-579	4.677%	$1,552

[Source: myFICO.com as of September 2016]

As you can see from this example, a borrower with top-level credit would pay $273 a month less than a consumer at the bottom rung of the credit ladder. That's an annual savings of $3,276 dollars, no small chunk of change. And when you think about that savings magnified over 30 years – to the tune of $98,280 – it's clear that it pays to protect your credit.

While you can call a credit-reporting agency, such as TransUnion and get your credit report, I think the best thing for consumers to do is to use www.myfico.com. Here's why: Not only will you learn what information is contained in your credit report, but you'll also get specific recommendations – straight from the horse's mouth, so to speak – on what specific steps you can take to improve your FICO® score over time. Plus, you'll learn how to *use* your credit score; and it's here where the www.myfico.com site is a most valuable resource.

At www.myfico.com, you'll find loads of information that tells you how to leverage your FICO® score to full advantage by shopping around for the best-rate loans. There are plenty of pointers on how to improve your credit standing, data about how lenders view consumers with similar credit profiles to yours, and even tips on how to guard your credit by thwarting identity theft. FICO® also offers an insightful, free 17-page online guide called "Understanding Your Credit Score," along with "myFICO Forums" an online community where you can post credit-related questions. Additionally, the FICO® score simulator – available online after you purchase your credit report – is a handy tool that lets you see the impact of certain actions on your credit score. For instance, using the FICO® score simulator, you can see how your credit score might improve (or worsen) if you do things like pay off all your debts, or (heaven forbid) miss a payment in the future.

Now let's turn to your VantageScores, something many of you may not be familiar with – but you should be.

What You Must Know About the New VantageScore

More than a decade ago, in March 2006, the "Big Three" credit reporting companies caused quite a stir when they announced that they had jointly developed a new credit score, called VantageScore. According to Equifax, Experian and TransUnion, this new score would be more "accurate" than existing credit scores, and would also provide far less variance in credit scores among the credit bureaus. For instance, one big complaint from consumers over the years is that they might get one credit score from Equifax – say it's 680, then another score of 710 from Experian, and a 740 score from TransUnion. With the VantageScore, consumers would supposedly benefit by getting scores that are much more similar because the three credit bureaus would all use the exact same methodology to calculate credit scores. Additionally, the "Big Three" came up with a new numerical and grading system to classify a person's credit, with credit scores ranging from 501 to 990 points. The breakdown for VantageScores originally looked like this:

VantageScore	Grade	Risk Category
901 to 990	A	Super Prime
801 to 900	B	Prime Plus
701 to 800	C	Prime
601 to 700	D	Non-Prime
501 to 600	F	High Risk

But more recently, VantageScores changed to the same numerical scale use by FICO – 300 to 850 points. So now your highest VantageScore can be 850 (not 990). But that doesn't mean those two scores from those two separate companies will be identical. Indeed, in September 2016 I checked my FICO score, and it was 795. My VantageScore, on the other hand, was 803. Not a huge disparity, but a difference nonetheless.

VantageScores – like FICO scores – have gone through multiple versions or iterations. We're now on the FICO 9 score and VantageScore 3.0.

VantageScore 3.0 is said to be the "most advanced, predictive credit scoring model" ever developed by VantageScore Solutions. VantageScore 3.0 uses reams of consumer data along with lender research to significantly expand the pool of people for whom credit scores can be generated.

Specifically, with VantageScore 3.0 between 27 million and 30 million adults who had previously been deemed as having "no credit files" or "too thin" credit files will now have credit scores created for them. According to VantageScore officials, outside of VantageScore 3.0, these consumers are simply "invisible to traditional scoring models."

Additionally, VantageScore Solutions says the VantageScore 3.0 is up to 25% more predictive than previous models, thanks to access to more granular data about consumers. In a nutshell, VantageScore 3.0 is better able to tell a lender whether prime and so-called "near prime" consumers are likely to pay their bills and credit obligations on time – or default on those financial responsibilities.

In rolling out the new credit score, VantageScore said it is also unveiling a "new VantageScore brand identity to support the new model as well as an all-new www.VantageScore.com website."

The VantageScore 3.0 model is being touted as much more consumer friendly, since the credit score introduces new plain-language reason code descriptions. To help explain "reason codes" to consumers, VantageScore also launched www.ReasonCode.org, a microsite aimed at further revealing why a consumer did not receive a better credit score.

Where To Get Free FICO or VantageScores

Once place to get your free FICO credit score or free VantageScore is from banks, credit unions and other lenders.

It makes sense that institutions that are responsible for dealing in finance and their customer's wealth should extend their financial knowledge to their clients.

So if you have a credit card through your bank, you can often view your FICO score or VantageScore by visiting:

- your account online, or
- FICO's Score Open Access program

A partial list of banks that offer this service and access to your credit scores include:

- American Express (FICO Score)
- CapitalOne (VantageScore)
- Citi (FICO Score)
- Chase (FICO Score)
- Discover (FICO Score)
- First Bankcard (FICO Score)
- Merrick Bank (FICO Score)
- USAA (VantageScore)

Have a checking account but no credit card? Don't despair. Some banks may allow you to view your FICO score or VantageScore. Check with your bank to see if this service is offered. Belong to a credit union? If so, you may have the same free access to your FICO score (depending on the institution). Check with your credit union to see if you can access this information. Some participating credit unions include:

- State Employees Credit Union of North Carolina (FICO Score)
- Pentagon Federal Credit Union (FICO Score)
- San Jose's Technology Credit Union (FICO Score)

Auto Loans and Student Loans

Are you currently financing your vehicle through an auto financing company? If so, you may be entitled to viewing your VantageScore or FICO score. A short list companies that participate include:

- Ally Financial (FICO Score)
- Lending Tree (VantageScore)
- RoadLoans

If you've recently gone to college or co-signed for your children's Sallie Mae Smart Option student loans, you are entitled to see your FICO score. You can log onto salliemae.com/landing/fico to access your score, as well as other pertinent information to your loan.

Credit Counselors

Finally, if you're looking for your free FICO score and expert insight to your credit history (and future), consider consulting a non-profit credit counselor. Their information is sourced from Experian, a credit-reporting agency, and through FICO's Score Open Access for Credit & Financial Counseling program. Consider contacting credit counselors at:

- Credit Builders Alliance
- The Financial Counseling Association of America
- Local Initiatives Support Corporation
- National Foundation for Credit Counseling

If you don't have Internet access to get your credit report and FICO® score, or if you prefer to deal directly with the credit agencies, call Equifax at 800-685-1111; Experian at 888-397-3742 and TransUnion at 800- 916-8800. Mailing addresses for these credit bureaus, as well as Innovis, are in **Appendix A**. (Read about Innovis at the end of this chapter. What you'll learn may shock you).

Now that you have some background information about why you should get your credit report and FICO® score or your VantageScore, let's talk about some of the biggest misconceptions regarding credit scores. As a consumer, your credit is of such critical importance that you can't afford to operate on the basis of false information. For starters, realize that you do have the power to upgrade your credit profile. Your credit score is something you can improve – with time and discipline. The following section tells you the real truth about credit scores.

Fact vs. Fiction about Credit Scores

FICTION: If I check my credit report often, all those "inquiries" will lower my credit score.

FACT: Your personal inquiries are called "soft" inquiries and do not impact your credit score at all. You can check your credit as much as you'd like with no negative impact, as long as you do it through a credit bureau or a company authorized to issue credit reports, such as myFICO.

EXPLANATION: Even though you may see all kinds of inquiries in your credit file, many of them have no bearing on your credit score. For instance, your credit score doesn't count your own inquiries, as well as those from existing creditors who are reviewing your account, or lenders trying to offer you "pre-approved" credit.

FICTION: I pay cash for everything and don't buy on credit or use credit cards, so my credit score should be excellent.

FACT: Having no credit history or never using credit can have a negative impact on your credit score.

EXPLANATION: It helps your credit score to have some history of paying credit obligations on time. Fair Isaac reports that people with no credit cards tend to be higher risk than those who have managed their debts responsibly.

FICTION: I'm going to close out my old accounts since I'm not using them anymore, and that will improve my credit score.
FACT: You can actually hurt your credit score by closing older, more "seasoned" accounts.
EXPLANATION: Generally speaking, it works in your favor to have older accounts in your credit file because it shows that you have a longer credit history.

FICTION: The most important factor in my credit score is whether or not I am "maxed out" on my credit cards.
FACT: The single biggest determinant of your credit score is how well you've paid your bills on time in the past.
EXPLANATION: Your credit scores take into account whether you've had late or missed payments, how far past due your bills were, how long ago the late pays occurred, and whether you have any collection items.

FICTION: My age, race, gender, marital status, income or where I live can impact my credit score.
FACT: None of those factors are taken into consideration at all when your FICO® credit score or VantageScore is determined.
EXPLANATION: Under U.S. law, it is illegal to for credit scoring to take into account race, age, color, nationality, religion, sex or marital status.

Because there is so much misinformation about what goes into your credit score, I thought you'd like to know directly from Fair Isaac how the company comes up with your FICO® score. In short, your credit file is reviewed and certain information about how you've managed your credit is statistically analyzed. Ultimately, five different categories are weighted to produce your FICO® score. Here's the breakdown of those five areas that contribute to your FICO® score:

What a FICO® Score Considers

1. **Payment History:** Approximately 35% of your score is based on this category.
2. **Amounts Owed:** About 30% of your score is based on this category.
3. **Length of Credit History:** Roughly 15% of your score is based on this category.
4. **Types of Credit in Use:** About 10% of your credit score is based on this category.
5. **New Credit:** Around 10% of your score is based on this category.

Is Credit Scoring Fair to Minorities?

Critics oppose credit scoring for two reasons. First, some argue that so much data collection intrudes on people's privacy. Also, some critics say that credit scoring discriminates against minorities. Fair Isaac officials dispute both assertions, especially the concept that credit scoring is unfair to minorities.

"Gender, race and nationality are factors that do not get added into the FICO scores," Ryan Sjoblad, a former Fair Isaac official told me when I originally wrote *Zero Debt*. "It knows nothing about you, except your credit-paying habits. It's hard to call it (credit scoring) racist, when it has no idea what your race is." To be honest, I agreed whole-heartedly – and most of you probably know that I'm African- American.

More recently, however, I have to say that I've come to believe that the issue is far more complex. It's not simply a matter of whether credit scores are racially biased. But if we pondered that issue, some experts would actually say "yes" they are.

Cathy O'Neill is a data scientist with a Ph.D. in mathematics from Harvard. She is also the author of the book *Weapons of Math Destruction: How Big Data Increases Inequality and Threatens Democracy*. O'Neill – a former hedge fund expert who now blogs at Mathbabe.org – makes a powerful argument about why it is very dangerous and, yes, *inherently biased* to rely on data analytics of the kind that are routinely used in credit scoring. O'Neill's assertion is essentially that the algorithms and mathematical models used by credit-scoring companies are only as good as the assumptions built into these statistical models. And therein, O'Neill says, is where the bias creeps in.

For instance, she says credit-scoring models are rooted in opinions, not just pure math and statistics. As O'Neill pus it: "Models are opinions embedded in mathematics." And exactly what opinions relate to credit-scoring models? She calls various models "Weapons of Math Destruction" or "WMDs" when they are opaque (i.e. not transparent) to their subjects; harmful to those affected by the model, and run at a huge scale. All of these descriptions apply to credit scoring models, especially poor people and minorities. As O'Neill writes: "Poor people are more likely to have bad credit and live in high-crime neighborhoods, surrounded by other poor people. Once ... WMDs digest that data, it showers them with subprime loans or for-profit schools." In short, O'Neill says disadvantaged populations face built in biases – like the assumption that everyone living in a certain zip code is higher risk and therefore should have higher insurance rates, financial fees or diminished access to credit. All these factors have credit, career and economic implications.

Little-Known Ways Your Credit Impacts You

Speaking of this, most people know that a poor credit score can impact your ability to get a mortgage, car, and credit cards. But did you know that your credit history has a much wider-ranging impact on you, far beyond your ability to obtain credit or loans?

"A lot of things are based on trust and your credit report, to some degree, talks about how trustworthy you are," says Eric Simons, a certified financial planner and head of Simons Financial Network in New York.

According to Simons and other experts, your credit history can also be legally considered if you're applying for automobile, medical or life insurance, are trying to rent a new apartment, or are seeking a new job or even a promotion at your existing place of employment.

Say you are up for a better-paying position at your company, one that would require you to manage a budget or deal with customer funds. Under the law, your bosses are entitled to check out your credit history as part of their evaluation of you – as long as they do it in accordance with the Fair Credit Reporting Act.

What this means is that they must first get your permission to check your credit. They must also inform you of your rights under the law. These rights include the right to dispute the accuracy or completeness of any information supplied by a credit reporting agency, and the right to a free consumer report upon request within 60 days. Also, if any of the information your employer obtains causes them to deny you a promotion or act "adversely" toward you, they must notify you in writing of which credit reporting agency they used.

The same notification requirements hold true for any insurance company that decides to terminate your policy, deny you insurance, or increase your rates, if such adverse action is taken based solely or partially on information in your consumer report.

Only a few states prohibit insures from using credit scores to set prices: California, Hawaii, and Massachusetts. In those states, insurers set premiums mostly on a consumer's driving record, the number of miles driven per year, and other factors.

How and When to Turn to the Credit Bureaus for Help

If you feel that something in your credit report is wrong, you can dispute it. You can also contest the erroneous info with the creditor. But you should first take some time to read up on and learn about a handful of other important rights under the Fair Credit Reporting Act (FCRA). You'll find more details about the FCRA in **Day 8** of *Zero Debt*. Briefly, among these rights granted to consumers are the following:

- **You can dispute inaccurate information contained in your file.**
  Once you tell a consumer-reporting agency that something in your file is wrong, that agency must investigate the item in

dispute, typically within 30 days. Ultimately, the credit agency must give you a written report summarizing the investigation. It must also provide you with an updated copy of your credit report if its investigation changes your report.

- **Erroneous information must be corrected or deleted.**
  But if something is correct, that data doesn't have to be removed unless it's outdated or can't be verified.

- **Only businesses with legitimate purposes can view your credit report – and then only with your permission.**
  For instance, in considering your application, a creditor, employer, landlord, insurer, or other such legitimate businesses can obtain information about you from a consumer-reporting agency.

The Credit Report You've Probably Never Heard Of

I've already told you how you can get a free copy of your credit file every 12 months from each of the "Big Three" credit-reporting agencies. But did you know that there's a fourth credit bureau of considerable influence in this country?

The company is called Innovis, and if you're wise, you'll definitely want to also contact Innovis and find out what information this company is reporting about you.

Back in 2003, Innovis denied that it was actually in the credit-reporting business. There are numerous published reports in which the company flat-out denied that the information it gathers or sells about consumers could be used by creditors for the purpose of extending credit. The company's tight-lipped policies caused NBC to warn consumers that "Innovis is a secret credit bureau that sells your credit information to companies that compile mailing lists for unsolicited mail, including charge cards."

Shortly thereafter, consumer advocates – like the Public Interest Research Group (PIRG) – started insisting that Innovis was in fact a credit bureau and should have to abide by the same rules as other credit agencies. After some outside pressure and scrutiny, Innovis now acknowledges that it is, indeed a credit reporting agency.

According to published reports, Innovis primarily collects negative information about consumers: things like late payments, judgments, bankruptcies, collection accounts, repossessions, and so forth. That information is then sold to banks and other financial institutions. Remember in **Day 1** when I advised you to stop the flood of credit offers coming to your home? Well, if you *do* get credit offers, you certainly want them to be the best ones available, like low interest rate balance transfers, for instance.

But when companies buy data from Innovis, reportedly what they are screening for is people with "bad" credit – or at least people who *used* to have bad credit. This can have two effects on you. First, it would screen you out of the lists of top-tier consumers who are getting low-interest credit offers. Second, it makes you fair game for a host of credit offers you probably don't want to get. Think about it for a minute: If a bank or credit card company is actively targeting consumers with poor credit histories, what kind of credit offers do you think they'll be making? More than likely, they'll be throwing out high interest-rate offers – above the 20% level – or solicitations for "secured" credit cards. Again if you're already considered a "sub-prime" borrower, you don't want to get these offers. So make sure you write Innovis and find out what information the company has about you.

You can obtain your Innovis credit report in four different ways:

1) **Online:** https://www.innovis.com/creditReport/index
2) **By phone:** 1-800-540-2505
3) **By mail:** write to this address:

Innovis Consumer Assistance
P.O. Box 1689
Pittsburgh, PA 15230-1689

4) **In person:** walk in at this address:

875 Greentree Road
8 Parkway Center
Pittsburgh, PA 15220

Because the online process is super speedy, I recommend using the website above rather than calling, using the mail service, or going in to Innovis's office. It will literally take you only about one minute to fill out the online form requesting your Innovis credit report. You'll supply your name, date of birth, current address, email, phone number and social security number. That's it. Fast, simple, and all done electronically.

The company will then immediately email you, providing you with three things: 1) a confirmation of your request; 2) a message saying you should get your Innovis credit report in the mail in a few business days; and 3) and link to a summary of your rights under the federal Fair Credit Reporting Act. (I'll explain that law and your rights under the FCRA, in layman's terms, in **Day 9**).

If you decide to skip the online method and instead use the mail, Innovis offers a simple, one-page form that you can obtain from its website. Alternatively, you can just send Innovis a letter asking for your credit file. Be sure to include your full name, date of birth, phone number, current address, email (if you have one), and Social Security number. For requests via mail, Innovis also requires two other items: 1) Proof of your current address (as verified by a copy of a government-issued ID, signed lease, recent utility bill, recent bank or credit union statement; and 2) Proof of Your Name (as documented by a government-issued ID, Social Security card, birth certificate, marriage license, Medicaid or Medicare card).

Just like the other three credit reporting firms, Innovis offers a free once-a-year report. You may also eligible for a free report if:

- Are unemployed and intend to apply for employment within the next 60 days.
- Receive public welfare assistance.
- Believe your file contains inaccurate information because of fraud.
- Have been denied credit, insurance, or other benefits within the last 60 days.

Additionally, if you've placed an Initial Fraud Alert on your Innovis Credit Report, you may receive one additional credit report in the 12 month period after you have placed the Initial Fraud Alert. If you placed an Extended Fraud Alert on your Innovis Credit Report, you may receive 2 free copies of your report during each 12 month period that the Extended Fraud Alert remains on your report.

If you do not meet the above requirements, an additional Innovis credit report can cost $1 to $11.50, depending on where you live. But those living in eight states/territories get another free credit report from Innovis, just as they can from the "Big Three" credit bureaus.

If You Live In:	Your 1st Report Is:	Your 2nd Report Is:
Colorado	Free	$8.00
Georgia	Free	Free
Maine	Free	$5.00
Maryland	Free	$5.00
Massachusetts	Free	$8.00
New Jersey	Free	$8.00
Puerto Rico	Free	$11.50
US Virgin Islands	$1.00	$1.00
Vermont	Free	$7.50

The rest of you must pay for a credit report from Innovis. Here is a breakdown of what you can expect to pay for that Innovis credit report, based on where you live:

California	$8.00
Connecticut	$5.00
Minnesota residents	$3.00
Montana residents	$8.50
All other states	$11.50

When you get your credit reports, if you see any bills or accounts that you left off the list of debts you created in **Day 3**, go ahead and add those debts to your list now. And just remember: the single-best thing you can do from this day forward to boost your credit standing is to *pay your bills on time.*

Day 5: Call your creditors & negotiate

Many people deep in debt may feel powerless to get their creditors to give them a break. But nothing could be further from the truth. Under the right circumstances, and armed with the right knowledge, you can win concessions from banks, credit card companies and others that you owe.

Your next step now is to use the list you created in **Day 3**, contact each creditor and ask for a lower interest rate. Depending on how much debt you have, doing this one step alone can save you hundreds, if not thousands of dollars – not to mention shave many months or years from the time you'll be paying off your debt.

You Have Leverage

Don't make the mistake of thinking that just because you owe money you don't have any power when it comes to dealing with credit card companies. The truth of the matter is you probably have far more leverage than you realize. If you've been making your payments on time (even if only the minimum amounts due), that credit-card company doesn't want to lose your business. So if you call and say that you have a better offer (or that you could get one) from another financial institution, they will probably lower your interest rate on the spot – or at least put your account under consideration for a rate reduction if you pay on time for, say, six months straight. They know it's a competitive market, and consumers get deluged with low-rate credit card and balance transfer options week after week. It's well worth it for a credit grantor to consider lowering your interest rate, rather than lose your business altogether because you initiate a balance transfer from another company.

Six Things to Ask For

Here are the main objectives when you call a creditor about your account. Depending on your circumstances, you want the person on the other end of the phone to do any or all of the following:

- Lower your interest rate
- Stop late fees
- Eliminate over-the-limit charges
- Upgrade your account to "current" status
- Remove a negative mark from your credit
- Accept a partial payment in lieu of the total due

Before you contact credit card companies, however, there is something I'd like to share with you to help you separate the myths from the facts when you get ready to negotiate.

The Biggest Myth about Credit Card Companies

I think the biggest myth about credit card companies is that they are big, impersonal institutions that aren't willing to budge in order to help consumers in financial trouble.

The reality is that credit card companies are run by individuals, and armed with the proper knowledge, perspective and strategy; you can get a lot of help from the right individual at these institutions.

Getting Your Creditors to Work with You

Probably the most productive thing you can do to get your creditors to work with you is to initiate the process. As painful as it might seem, yes, I want you to actually pick up the phone and *call them* – instead of the other way around. I know some of you have gotten used to ducking telephone calls from banks and department stores, asking your kids or family members to fib and say you aren't home, or disguising your voice to avoid dealing with your creditors. But beginning today, you're going to be proactive about knocking out your debts. And it starts with you figuring out a workable plan – something that works for the creditor, but something that you can also live with.

Be frank about your situation. If you have recently lost your job, are going through a divorce, have gotten sick and been unable to work, or whatever, let your creditors know about it. Again, part of your strategy (yes, it's a strategy, but you only want to say what is honest and accurate) is to appeal to that person's sense of fairness and compassion. After all, you are dealing with another human being – even though some people who've been browbeaten by debt collectors might argue otherwise.

Now, I realize that it's not always realistic or practical to rely on someone else's willingness to help you out of a bind. In fact, I've heard horror stories about consumers who tried to work out financial arrangements, only to be berated by debt collectors that used foul language and clearly had no compassion whatsoever. I'm not talking right now about dealing with collection agencies – they're a different story. I'm referring to your direct negotiations with creditors, like Visa, MasterCard, or Sears.

What's The Impact of a 16.9% Interest Rate?

Assume you want your credit card company to lower your interest rate – maybe from 16.9% to 5.9%.

To figure the simple annual interest on any debt, take the total amount you owe and multiply it by the interest rate, expressed as a decimal. HINT: To get the rate shown as a decimal, just move the decimal point over two places to the left.

So let's say you have a $3,000 Visa bill at 16.9% interest. If you're not aggressive about knocking this debt out, that $3,000 balance will take 16 years and 7 months to pay off. Why? You'll pay about $60 a month, assuming you only make minimum payments on your outstanding balance.

Annual Interest: $507

Let me show you how I got the annual interest of $507.

The formula for figuring simple annual interest is:

Amount owed ($3,000) x Interest rate (shown as a decimal) (.169)

(<u>REMEMBER</u>: to show the 16.9% interest rate as a decimal, I just moved the decimal point over two places to the left.)

So $3,000 x .169 = $507
Annual Interest = $507

But What If You Had A 5.9% Interest Rate?

You'd pay a lot less in finance charges and ...
You could knock out this debt in just one year.
Here's how:

New Annual Interest: $177
Your original debt of $3,000 plus $177 in annual interest totals $3,177. To get rid of that $3,177 in a year, you'd need to pay $264.75 a month, since:

<u>$3,177 (total debt)</u> = $264.75 (required monthly payment) 12 (months)

In this example, negotiating to get a better interest rate would give you the ability to pay off this debt in one year instead of 16 years; and the lower 5.9% rate would also save you thousands of dollars in interest charges over time.

By the way, which way do you want interest to flow in your life? Realize that as a consumer, all you do is pay interest. Once you get financially fit and start saving and investing, you start to collect interest. Once you truly get the concept of interest, you'll probably agree with this statement:

Those who understand interest are destined to **collect** *it; those who don't are doomed to* **pay** *it for life.*

That statement is really just a variation of what the Bible teaches. Proverbs 22:7 says: "Just as the rich rule the poor, *so the borrower is servant to the lender*" (my emphasis added). So when you borrow, you become a slave, of sorts, to your creditor.

What's the Best Time to Negotiate with Creditors?

It's almost always better to deal with creditors *before* you actually miss a payment. Creditors are much more willing to work with you if you've paid your bills on time. They're trusting that you'll continue to honor your obligations – even if it means paying only minimum payments, or even less than the minimums, if that's an agreement that you stick with.

If your credit is already shot, it's often more advantageous to negotiate with creditors after the debt you owe is so old that the creditor has practically forgotten about it.

What do I mean by this? Let's look at the two following scenarios:

Say you lose your job unexpectedly. Statistics show that it's not easy – or fast – to find a replacement job. On average, it will take about one month to replace every $10,000 in income lost. Therefore, if you were among the top wage-earners in this country, and you had a six-figure job paying $100,000, it will probably take you about 10 months to find a similar-paying job. Likewise, if you were earning $40,000 a year, on average, it will take you four months to find a comparable-paying position. In the meantime, if you don't think you can pay all your bills, start calling your creditors immediately. Ask them to lower your interest rate, even if only temporarily. Again, credit card companies and other lenders are much more willing to be flexible for people who take the time to *initiate the process* of working out a payment plan, a reduced interest deal, or whatever.

But let's say you have an old debt – a $2,000 bill that you racked up three years ago from a department store. For whatever reason, you never paid that bill and the store has already reported your non-payment on your credit report. The department store has also "written off" your account as a "bad debt expense." So if you come along now and offer to make a lump sum payment as a settlement in lieu of payment in full, chances are the creditor will go for it. After all, that company would rather get some money from you, than no money at all. If you work out one of these deals, however, make sure you get the creditor to first agree in writing that it will *completely delete* the negative history from your credit report if you send in the agreed-upon payment.

If a creditor just marks your past due account as "Paid" or "Paid as Agreed," that may do absolutely nothing for your credit score. They have to also agree to delete any references to late payments that they may have previously put on your credit report. Never let them "upgrade" your account status to "Paid Collection" or "Paid Charge-Off." Negative information can legally stay in your credit file for seven years, based on the date of "last activity." So changing your account to "Paid Charge-Off" restarts the clock, adding another

7-year negative mark to your file. Look at **Appendix B** for a Sample Settlement Letter to creditors to get them to agree to a settlement and remove negative marks from your credit file.

13 Negotiating Strategies to Lower Your Interest Rate, or Eliminate Late Fees and Over-The-Limit Charges

- **Call in the morning**

  Don't call at the end of the day when customer service representatives are tired, more stressed and have been dealing all day with irate cardholders. Also avoid calling on the weekends; there may not be a supervisor there if you need one. Be aware of time-zone differences, as 9am on the West Coast is 12pm EST, a typical time for a less-staffed lunch.

- **Be polite in making any requests**

  Get the conversation off to a good start by using good manners. Say *"hello"* or *"good morning"* to the person you're talking to and call her by name, as in *"Good morning, Susan, this is Kim Jones, I'm calling about my account."* Make sure your tone sounds like you are making requests, not demands. Be friendly and conversational, not adversarial, to establish a good rapport and get the cooperation of the person on the other end of telephone.

- **Request to speak to a supervisor if necessary**

  If you get nowhere with the person you're talking to, don't be afraid to "escalate" your phone call by asking to speak with a supervisor. Even if the conversation isn't confrontational or negative, you may require a manager because some employees will say they don't have the power to honor your request.

- **Point out your length of time as a customer**

  For those of you who've been with a credit card company for a number of years, use your long-term status as leverage in asking for what you want. This can really work in your favor, because most banks value loyal, long-term customers; they don't want to lose them.

- **Emphasize how much business you've done**

  Many of you might have racked up a lot of charges over time. If you've been a valued customer by virtue of having charged many goods and services, make that known. And state that you also value the relationship with your creditor and would like to remain a customer in good standing.

- **Stress your willingness pay what you owe**

  Creditors may not be inclined to be flexible with individuals they perceive as trying to "get one over." The worst thing you can do is to convey the impression that you're a "deadbeat" who is out to weasel out of paying your obligations. A better strategy: stress that you are, in fact, willing and desirous of paying your bills.

- **Reveal any extenuating circumstances**

  In cases where there have been out-of-the-ordinary circumstances, let your creditors know this. For instance, if you lost your job, suffered a death in the family or something major happened in your life that caused you to miss a payment, tell them. Also make it clear if something happened that prevented you from getting your bills, such as you moved addresses or got divorced and your ex got the statements. Creditors may be willing to waive late fees in such cases.

- **Directly refer to your credit report**

  Don't be ashamed to say that a negative mark from the creditor could hurt your credit report – especially if you're in the market for a new car or house. Tell them your situation, and say something like, *"I'd hate for this one blemish from your company to damage my credit standing or my ability to get a loan."* Tip: only do this with your original creditors, who will likely be more sensitive to your predicament. Don't try this tactic with collection agents. That's giving them too much information, and they'll just turn that information against you, saying, in effect: "If you don't pay up, you won't get that new house."

- **Make "first-time" cases work in your favor**

  If you've never been late before or you've never had an over-the limit fee assessed, ask directly for a removal of a late fee or over-the-limit charge. A little-known fact is that many credit card companies give their employees the option (without even getting a supervisor's approval) of waiving late fees once every 12 months. If this is the case for you, do ask to get those fees removed. You might be surprised at how easily they will agree.

- **Mention their competition**

  As a last resort, when you're negotiating for a lower interest rate, mention that you might be inclined to take your business elsewhere. The point here is not to make an idle threat. And I wouldn't start the conversation off with talk about you possibly going to a competitor. But you'd certainly be justified in exploring your options – and telling the creditor about other companies' balance transfer deals or lower interest-rate offers – if they won't budge on high interest rate cards.

- **Document all conversations in writing**

  In the event you have to go back and get something corrected, or removed, it helps your case if you can refer to your written notes and say, *"I spoke to XYZ person on this date, and was told such and such."*

- **Initiate requests immediately**

  Anytime you see there's an issue you want resolved, contact your creditor immediately. Don't wait a couple of weeks, or even worse, a few months to ask for a rate reduction or removal of late fees. That works against you because it seems like you didn't care enough about the situation to do take instant action. It also reflects well on you when you initiate the call regarding late payments, instead of waiting for them to contact you.

- **Explain online payment discrepancies**

  If you were paying a bill online and for some reason payment didn't go through, that could be a legitimate reason for late fees to get removed. Another possibility: say you were making minimum payments on a credit card that had a teaser rate of 0% interest for six months. And assume you were paying $100 a month on that card via automatic online payments. Six months later, your teaser rate expired and the normal 14.9% rate kicked in. All of a sudden, your new minimum payment might be $115 a month. If you weren't keeping up with things, you would still be automatically sending in $100 payments online. The first time that happened, you'd likely get dinged with a late payment, for being $15 short in your payment. If you call the credit card company and point this out to them, they'll look at your online payment history and will likely waive the late fee - once.

These techniques work. How do I know? I've used some of them, and have talked to many others, like Greg Lackowitz, who have successfully used these strategies. Lackowitz works at a television station in New York. He once called Discover and was able to get the interest on his credit card reduced from 18.9% to 7.9%.

Day 6: Switch cards if necessary

If you have any creditors who won't budge on cards with sky-high interest rates (perhaps because you've missed a payment or two), be willing to switch the balance to a new card, if you can. To find good rates, get online and get a better deal. Start by visiting www.cardratings.com or log onto www.creditcardperks.com.

The Benefit of Comparison Shopping

I love these sites because they really empower consumers who are willing to comparison shop, which can really save you money and help you get a tailored credit card that addresses your circumstances. For example, at CardRatings.com, an award-winning website, you'll find helpful articles on everything from how to educate your child about credit cards to credit cards that make the most sense for students or small business owners. The founder of CardRatings.com is Curtis Arnold, the author of *How You Can Profit from Credit Cards: Using Credit to Improve Your Financial Life and Bottom Line*. CardRatings.com also puts out a free email newsletter that includes reviews of the best rated cards.

Meanwhile, you'll find a column written by yours truly at CreditCardPerks.com, where I explain how to manage credit cards wisely – as well as get all the perks and benefits possible (like cash back or free travel) out of prudent credit-card use.

Warnings about Obtaining New Credit

One caveat, though: I don't recommend opening up a slew of new credit card accounts – even if you get multiple teaser offers with initial low interest rates. Opening up too many accounts at once can actually hurt your credit score, for two reasons. For starters, remember that length of credit history is one factor (approximately 15%) in determining your FICO® score. Generally speaking, the longer you have been managing credit, the more positively that influences your score. So if you open several new accounts, the average age of your accounts will decrease, possibly lowering your score.

Additionally, you don't want to have too many inquiries on your credit report. While you're shopping around for a better rate, try to do it all within a 14-day period. Fair Isaac says that it counts multiple inquiries made around the same time frame – say, for a new credit card or a new auto loan – as one single inquiry, so as not to penalize consumers who are comparison shopping. Also, your FICO® score ignores all inquiries made in the 30 days before scoring, just to ensure that your score won't be lowered as a result of you hunting for the best deals. Moreover, some of the latest versions of FICO® scoring software count auto and mortgage inquiries within a 45-day period as one inquiry. Still, to be on the safe side, it's probably best to shop around for that new car or new home within a 14-day timeframe, because you can't be sure that your lender has the most up-to-date FICO® scoring software.

It's also important to realize the limitations of inquiries. "Hard" credit inquiries occur when you apply for credit (such as a credit card, auto loan or mortgage) and the bank pulls your credit file. This "hard" inquiry will still stay on your credit report for two years. The good news is that a "hard" inquiry only counts against you for the first 12 months. After that, it's not taken into consideration when calculating your FICO® score.

Another insider tip: don't believe it when people say that getting rid of your credit cards will improve your credit. Closing your credit card accounts almost never helps your score and most likely will hurt it.

Here's the bottom line: Don't open a barrage of new credit card accounts. But having one new account with a single digit interest rate – or perhaps a 0% offer for six months or a year – can save you big bucks. Also, don't just close out or cancel all your old credit card accounts, which, as noted, might reduce your credit score.

Day 7: Always exceed the minimum payment due

For many years, creditors typically asked that you pay about 2% of your outstanding balance. That was a great way for them to get rich, because it meant you'd be a customer for life, taking many years to pay off goods and services you charged ages ago. If you can swing it, I recommend always paying at least two, preferably three times the required minimum amount due.

But a while back some of you may have noticed a change in your credit card bills. The minimum payments your bank required went up. What happened is that regulators got really concerned about consumers being caught in a cycle of debt as a result of only making minimum payments on their credit cards. Therefore, the Office of the Comptroller of the Currency mandated that banks force you to pay a minimum payment that would knock out not just interest, but also some of the principal balance due on your credit cards. The result is that most of the major credit card companies raised their required minimum payment from 2% to 4% of your balance. Financial institutions, including Bank of America, MBNA, and Citibank announced that they were doubling the minimum payments required by their customers. The Bankruptcy Abuse Prevention and Consumer Protection Act of 2005 also required credit card companies to put a notice on your monthly statements saying how long you'd be in debt if you only make the minimum payments. These days, most credit card companies are back to charging minimum payments averaging around 2% of credit card balances.

For some of you, I have no doubt that when you wake up and start to see how long you could be financially beholden to a credit card company, it will be a huge shock to your system. Even more to the point, some of you may be scared witless at how much your credit cards payments keep going up – especially if you're not seeing the balances go down substantially.

Well, there's good and bad news to this whole new era of higher minimum payments. The bad news is that you may have to do some serious belt-tightening in order to afford to make your credit card payments and juggle all your other monthly bills. If you're having troubles, you could try to negotiate a lower rate to give yourself some breathing room. (*See my negotiating tips in* **Day 5**). You might also consider tapping the equity in your home, if you're a homeowner, to pay off high-rate credit card debt with lower-rate mortgage debt, which is tax deductible. Before taking this route, though, be sure to read by advice on this topic in **Day 23**. Only certain people should swap credit card debt for mortgage debt. And if you're not careful, this strategy can backfire. The good news about higher credit card minimums is that by forcing you to cough up bigger chunks of money in the short run, they will get you out of debt faster in the long run.

Minimum Payments Now Really Equal Maximum Payments, in the Long-Run

Paying so-called minimum payments now actually ends up costing you more – a lot more – over the long haul. The math behind some of the calculations that determine your interest rate can be tricky. And I won't get into all the complex, and sometimes mind-boggling formulas that are used to calculate your Annual Percentage Rate (APR). But suffice to say that for every $1,000 you owe, if you paid a minimum of say 3%, you'd only be paying $30 a month. With just $2,500 in debt on a card with an 18% interest rate, you'd spend more than10 years paying it off at 3% ($75/month) and you'd pay more than $2,100 in finance charges on top of what you originally spent.

A Guaranteed Investment Return

Many charge cards carry very high interest rates of 15% to 21%, or more. If you carry large credit card balances, that's a drain on your monthly finances. At the very least, start doubling up on your payments in order to pay off those credit cards sooner, rather than later. If you pay off a MasterCard that is charging you 21% interest, that's the equivalent to earning a guaranteed 21% investment return – and you won't find that kind of guarantee anywhere in the stock market.

But I Don't Have the Money!

I know some of you may be saying: "I don't have the money! If I had the money to pay three times my minimum balance – or even all of it, I would've done it by now!" Well, keep reading – particularly in **Day 15** through **Day 24** – for ideas about how you're going to come up with the money to ultimately achieve Zero Debt status. For now, to get you on track, I want you to write a check this day to *pay more than the minimum due* on one credit card that you owe. I don't care if it's a $5 check. Just pay extra money on any one bill right now. It can be on a card you've already paid this month or an upcoming bill. But mail that check *today*!

Week 2 Overview

This week, you will:

- √ Dispute any inaccuracies in your credit file
- √ Educate yourself about your legal rights
- √ Halt creditor harassment
- √ Guard against identity theft to shield your credit
- √ Set up a good filing and record-keeping system
- √ Face the truth about your financial situation
- √ Create SMART financial goals

Day 8: Dispute any inaccuracies in your credit file

The FACT ACT, also called the Fair and Accurate Credit Transactions Act, gives you the right to obtain your credit file free of charge. Under a federal law called the Fair Credit Reporting Act, you also have the right to have erroneous information deleted from your credit report. So, if anything is wrong in your credit file, just write the credit bureaus at the addresses found at the end of this book, and state your dispute. Errors include closed accounts that are still shown as open, data about accounts you did not open, or negative items, such as bankruptcies or liens, possibly from someone else with a similar name or social security number. The credit bureaus have 30 days to investigate your claims. After that, they must remove any information that is found to be inaccurate or that can no longer be verified.

How Accurate Are Credit Reports?

According to a number of consumer groups in the United States, many credit reports are filled with inaccuracies. According to the latest study from the Federal Trade Commission (FTC):

- 1 in 5 Americans have a mistake in their credit reports
- 5.2% of the group studied had a mistake significant enough to result in higher interest rates
- Nearly 13% of the studied group experienced a change in their FICO credit scores as a result of successfully challenging an error in one or more of their credit reports
- 6.3% of those with errors saw their scores increase by one to 19 points after they challenged reporting errors; 2.1% saw a 25 to 49 point increase and 2.3% had a 50 to 99 point increase

How Do Mistakes In Your Credit File Occur?

Many errors in your credit report revolve around the fact that the information listed about you is not complete, is not updated, or actually describes someone else. Mistakes in your credit file can happen in any number of ways, but most of them are the result of human error. For instance, you might accidentally give someone the wrong social security number. Or maybe an administrative assistant or salesman read your social security number incorrectly on an application, or typed it in wrong on a computer.

In other cases, errors in your credit file can occur if you apply for credit under different names (i.e. William Johnson, Bill Johnson, etc.) Sometimes family members get their credit histories crisscrossed, as when a Joe Jones Senior finds that his credit file erroneously contains some of Joe Jones Junior's credit information. "It's amazing how many times Juniors and Seniors get mixed up," an ex FICO official told me, who also used to work for a credit-reporting company, and saw credit file errors first-hand.

Credit Errors Can Cost You Money and More

No matter how the mistake occurs, errors in your credit report can cost you money, as illustrated above by the study conducted by the Consumer Federation of America and the National Credit Reporting Association. With incorrect information in your credit file, you also run the risk of being denied basic services – like utilities or cell phone service – as well as more crucial things, like getting insurance or a new job.

Fixing Errors & Cleaning Up Your Credit File

Some errors can be dealt with immediately. Others require a serious letter-writing campaign. Start out by going directly to your creditor and requesting that they delete outdated or negative information that is inaccurate from your credit report. Sometimes it may just take contacting your creditor directly to overturn the mistake. If it seems like a more-involved error, or you can't get any help from the original creditor, contact the major credit bureaus directly and file disputes.

Technically, you have two options when filing a dispute: you can contact either the credit bureau, or you can contact the **data furnisher** (the company that provides information to each bureau). For a quicker response, the data furnisher may be your best option, but they aren't legally obligated to pursue every type of dispute and most only accept disputes through the mail.

Contacting the credit bureaus directly allows you have the convenience of applying online, it adds a legally-binding statement to help clear your name to your creditors, and they're legally obligated to contact the institutions (including the data furnishers) that are affected by the error. The catch is that the dispute may take 30 – 45 days, though many are resolved within two weeks.

Raising Your FICO® Score

Getting rid of mistakes in your credit file can raise your FICO score, because your score is based on the information contained in your credit report(s). Some simple strategies to raise your FICO score include:

- Pay your bills on time and keep them up to date
- Keep your balances as low as possible on credit cards and other "revolving" credit accounts

- Pay down your debt, rather than moving it around
- Refrain from opening a rash of accounts all at once
- Secure new credit selectively, and over time, to re-establish credit if you've had difficulties in the past

Improve Your Credit Score in 3 Days – Legally

If you're applying for a mortgage, and you think an error on your credit report will get you turned down or cause you to pay a higher interest rate, you *must* read my advice in **Day 23**. I'll reveal a legitimate way you can quickly raise your credit score. It's called "Credit Re-Scoring" and it's a legal, fast way to fix errors in your credit file and improve your credit standing – in most cases in as little as two or three days. The National Association of Mortgage Brokers started this rapid dispute process in 1998, after its members saw how many errors in credit reports were preventing borrowers from getting loans, or forcing them to paying unfairly high interest rates.

Day 9: Educate yourself about your legal rights

As a consumer, you have a multitude of rights under the law, as it pertains to your debt. Some rights are based on recent legislation; other rights stem from laws that are decades old. Let's start with newly-passed initiatives you need to know.

In 2009, the U.S. House of Representatives passed the CARD Act, which was initially proposed as the Credit Cardholders' Bill of Rights Act. This pro-consumer bill was designed to end what consumers and critics say are abusive and unfair credit card practices by the banking industry. For instance, under the Credit Cardholders' Bill, banks would have to give you 45-days' notice before they increase your interest rate – as opposed to the current 15 days' notice. The bill would also put an end to questionable late fees, require better disclosure of credit card terms and conditions, and prevent banks from arbitrarily hiking your credit card interest rate just because your credit score drops.

In addition to the CARD Act, perhaps the strongest measure that you need to know is the Fair Debt Collection Practices Act, also known as Public Law 95-109. Passed in 1977, this law protects consumers from harassment, abuse or unfair actions by collection agencies.

When your account goes so far past due that your creditor doesn't think it's likely that you'll pay up, that creditor will often write your debt off as un-collectable. To get some money, however, the creditor can sell your debt to a third party collection agency, or hire that collection agency to work on a commission basis to try to recover some of the money you owe.

By the time a debt collector enters the picture, as you may know, your credit has already taken a hit. But here's where it can get really nasty.

Debt collection firms have been known to use every tactic under the sun – including legal and illegal means – to force consumers to pay their bills. If a collection agency comes after you, you may be subjected to any or all of the following things:

- coercion
- threats
- lies/deception
- intimidation
- fear
- blackmail
- harassment
- constant phone calls

It may or may not surprise you to learn that all of these tactics are ILLEGAL. For example, creditors can't claim that you will be arrested, curse at or verbally threaten you, or call you at all hours (such as before 8 a.m. and after 9 p.m. your local time) – even though such ploys are common, according to John Bowe, a former collection agent from Hempstead, New York, who is now a police officer in Georgia.

"If the debt collector realizes that they debtor is ignorant of the law, he'll try to skirt the law," says Bowe, who's seen it all.

10 Rights Protecting Consumers

There are 10 major areas within the Fair Debt Collections Practice Act that are designed to safeguard your rights. Read this chapter carefully. It will arm you with virtually everything you need to know in order to end any illegal debt collection practices you might be enduring. The bottom line is that just because you owe money, that doesn't give debt collection firms the right to treat you unfairly. Here are the 10 safeguards for consumers:

1. **How Creditors Track You Down**

   This area of the law is formally called "Acquisition of Location Information." It basically limits what debt-collectors can legally do to find you. For instance, debt collectors:

   - Can't tell third parties, such as your boss or neighbors, that they're trying to reach you about a debt
   - Shall only say to others that they're trying to confirm or correct your location (and not mention your debt)
   - Must not communicate with anyone else (like your supervisor) more than once, unless the debt collector believes the location information given was erroneous or incomplete
   - Are not supposed to mail you anything via postcard, either at home or at your place of employment
   - Can't use any kind of mailing, envelope, or other communication that would let someone else know that the company is a debt collection agency
   - Are prohibited from contacting you once you notify them in writing that you are represented by an attorney and give them the attorney's name/address

2. **The Way Debt Collectors Communicate about You**

   This area of the law prevents collection agencies from hounding you or trying to embarrass you by telling others your personal business. The law states that debt collectors:

   - Can't communicate with you before 8 a.m. or after 9 p.m. (your local time) unless you give them permission or they have a court order to do so
   - Can't contact you if you've notified them that a lawyer is representing you

- Can't call you on the job if you tell them that your employer prohibits you from receiving such calls.
- Can't talk about your situation with anyone; not your friends, relatives, neighbors or co-workers. The only ones they can discuss your debts with are your attorney, the original creditor and credit- reporting agencies.

3. **Prohibitions Against Harassment or Abuse**

No debt collector is legally allowed to harass, abuse or oppress you – under any circumstances, whatsoever. Any of the following tactics are violations of the Fair Debt Collection Practices Act:

- The use of violence, or the threat of it, or any criminal action that would hurt a person's body, property or reputation
- Obscene or profane language (oral or written)
- Publishing any lists (except to a credit bureau) that shows consumers who refused to pay a debt
- Threatening or actually posting the debt for sale to another party in order to compel repayment
- Constantly calling an individual on the telephone or engaging a consumer in repeated conversations with the intention to annoy, abuse or harass someone

4. **False or Misleading Representations**

Collection agencies are prohibited from making false or misleading representations to consumers in the course of trying to secure debt repayment. Some violations of the law in this area include:

- Falsely stating or implying that the debt collector is bonded by, or associated with, any federal or state government entity

- Falsely representing the nature of any debt, the amount owed, the legal status of the account, or compensation paid to the collection agency for recovering the debt
- Falsely claiming that the debt collector is an attorney or represents an attorney
- Falsely asserting that you will be imprisoned or arrested if you don't pay your bills (debtors' prisons don't exist anymore in this country)
- Falsely representing that your failure to pay could result in your wages being garnished, your property being seized, or your assets being sold – unless such measures are lawful, and unless the debt collector actually intends to take those actions
- Falsely stating such misinformation as the documents they send to you represent a legal process or that the debt collector works for a credit bureau

5. **Unfair Practices**

No debt collector can use dishonest or unfair means of making you pay your debts. The following actions are deemed to be violations of the law:

- Collecting any money at all – such as interest, late fees or charges other than the principal amount – unless it is specifically permitted by law and/or authorized by the agreement that created the debt
- Taking post-dated checks from you that are more than five days away, unless the debt collector informs you between 3 to 10 business days before depositing the check
- Soliciting postdated checks for the purpose of threatening or instituting criminal prosecution

- Depositing or threatening to deposit any postdated check before the date of such check
- Making collect calls to consumers, or doing anything that would cause debtors to incur charges for communication by debt collectors who are trying to conceal the purpose of their contact

6. **Validation of Debts**

As a consumer, you have the right to verify, validate or dispute any debt you are told about, within a given time frame. Within five days of initially contacting you, a debt collection agency must:

- Send you a written notice containing the amount of the debt, the name of the credit, a statement informing you of your right to dispute it within 30 days, and a statement indicating that if you contest any portion of the debt, the debt collector will obtain verification of the debt and mail it to you
- Supply you with the name and address of the original creditor, if different from the current creditor (if you ask for this information in writing)
- Cease collection attempts during the "verification of debt" period, if you dispute the debt or ask for the name and address of the original creditor

7. **Multiple Debts**

The law protects your repayment rights when you owe multiple debts to creditors. In this case, debt collectors:

- May not apply any payments you make to any debt that you dispute

- Must follow your instructions about how you want debts repaid (i.e., which debt should be paid first on your outstanding balances)

8. Legal Action by Debt Collectors

Federal law limits where debt collectors can bring legal proceedings against consumers who owe money. In general, any debt collector initiating legal action shall:

- Bring legal action against real property only in a judicial district or similar legal entity where the property is located
- Barring the above provision, debt collectors can bring action in the judicial district where the consumer signed the contract or where he/she currently lives

9. Furnishing Certain Deceptive Forms

Debt collection agencies are prohibited from supplying you with misleading or deceptive forms in a bid to make you pay your debts. The Fair Debt Collections Reporting Act states that it is unlawful for:

- Debt collectors to design compile or furnish any form knowing that such a form would create a false belief or a false impression that anyone other than the debt collection agency is participating in the collection activity (for example, debt collectors can't falsely claim lawyers or government agencies are involved)

10. **Civil Liability**

When debt collectors break the law, they can be sued for failing to abide by federal rules, and forced to pay:

- The actual damages sustained
- Additional damages up to $1,000 (for an individual)
- The lesser of $500,000 or 1% of the debt collector's net worth (in the case of a class action lawsuit)

If you believe a debt collection firm has violated any of these laws in dealing with you, report the company at once to your state Attorney General's office and the Federal Trade Commission at www.ftc.gov or 877-FTC-HELP.

And make no mistake, in addition to breaches of the Fair Debt Collections Practices Act, violations of the Fair Credit Reporting Act also happen. For instance, Pennsylvania-based NCO Group, which is one of America's biggest debt collection firms, agreed in May 2004 to pay regulators what was then a record $1.5 million to settle charges brought by the Federal Trade Commission that NCO Group routinely violated the FCRA by reporting inaccurate information about consumer accounts to credit- reporting agencies. That $1.5 million settlement had been the largest-ever civil penalty ever obtained in a FCRA case. The settlement also required NCO to implement a monitoring program to review all complaints received and make sure that reporting errors are corrected quickly.

Later, in 2006, ChoicePoint Inc. agreed in a separate case to pay $10 million to settle claims under the FCRA. To date, that is still the largest such settlement of its kind, but it didn't put a halt to bad behavior and egregious violations of federal credit laws.

More recently, in 2014, Telecheck Services Inc. of Houston and its debt-collection entity, TRS Recovery Services, Inc., agreed to pay $3.5 million to settle Federal Trade Commission charges that they violated the Fair Credit Reporting Act. That agreement came on the heels of another case in which Certegy Check Services also settled with the FTC and was slapped with a $3.5 million penalty for violating the FCRA. In both of these cases, regulators accused the check-cashing companies of not following proper dispute procedures, refusing to investigate consumers' credit disputes, and failing to fix errors on people's credit reports. Other companies were fined in 2015 and 2016.

As a consumer, you have to stand up for yourself when dealing with debt collectors. Yes, you may owe money, but that doesn't give them the right to harass or treat you unfairly.

One final tip: if you agree to payment arrangements, never send postdated checks to a collection agency. "Instead, send in money orders," suggests Bowe, the ex-collection agent. He says collection agencies have been known to deposit checks earlier than agreed, or to "accidentally or intentionally" debit your checking account for an amount higher than what was agreed. Either way, if there's a mix-up, "now you have to fight to get your money back, and that might be a slow process," says Bowe.

Day 10: Stop collection agency harassment

If any debt collection firms are harassing you – and you now know from the previous chapter that harassment is illegal – you can make them stop immediately.

"Cease Contact" or "Cease and Desist" Letter

Simply write a two-sentence letter advising them to cease all contact with you. The first sentence should say: *"I am unable to pay this bill because..."* or *"I refuse to pay this debt because..."* and explain your reason. You also have the option of not providing a reason at all. The second sentence should state: *"I hereby assert my right, under Section 805-C of the Fair Debt Collection Practices Act, to request that you cease any further communication with me."* In **Appendix C** of *Zero Debt*, you will find a sample Cease & Desist Letter. This basic language is all you need to say to debt collectors to get them off your back.

After they receive your "Cease & Desist" letter, debt collection firms can't contact you, except to indicate that the collection process against you has stopped, or that they plan to take, or recommend that your original creditor take, legal action against you, such as taking you to court. Even then, debt collectors can't threaten legal action unless they *truly* intend to take it. Either way, the annoying phone calls and those harassing letters will immediately end.

"Usually (collectors) will say they'll proceed with court action and it's not true," says former collection agent John Bowe. "They'll say things like 'Your wages will be garnished 'even if it's not true, because collectors will walk right over a person who's ignorant of the law. Knowing the Fair Debt Collections Practices Act is the debtor's best tool against collection agents."

Using the U.S. Post Office

When you send your "Cease & Desist" letter, make absolutely sure that you send it Certified Mail, Return Receipt Requested. I can't stress enough the importance of taking this step. "You definitely want to send the letter certified mail," cautions Bowe. "If it's not sent certified, they'll probably say it got lost in the mail and contact you again."

Your Certified Mail receipt from the Post office will be your proof of mailing. And having that Return Receipt – signed by an employee at the collection agency – will bolster your claims if you get embroiled in a legal dispute.

I don't care how broke you are; don't send off any Cease & Desist Letters if they're not processed through the U.S. Postal Service as Certified Mail-Return Receipt Requested. Otherwise, you'll be sorry. And you'll have wasted your time. As of this writing, to send a letter Certified Mail will cost you $3.30, in addition to your postage charges. To get proof of delivery, you must fill out Form 3811 (the green Return Receipt form) at the Post Office. That will cost you $2.70. Again, don't fret over these charges; it's money well spent. Obviously, postal rates are subject to be raised over time. So for the latest, up-to-date fees, please visit the U.S. Postal Service website at: http://www.usps.gov.

Day 11: Prevent identity theft to protect your credit

Identity theft is a very serious and growing problem in the United States. Identity theft occurs when someone steals your private information, such as your driver's license or Social Security number, and uses that data for his or her own personal gain, to open credit accounts, get bogus tax refunds, or take out loans in your name.

How big of a problem is identity theft? It depends on whom you ask. Some research shows that hundreds of thousands of people annually are victimized by identity theft; other data suggest that ID theft affects millions of individuals each year.

For instance, more than 3 million complaints by consumers were filed with the Federal Trade Commission in 2015, with more than 490,000 complaints, or 16%, directly related to identity theft. And even though identity theft was the second-most common consumer complaint in 2015 (behind debt collection), prior to 2015 ID theft had been the top reported complaint for 15 years in a row, FTC data show.

Remember, however, these numbers reflect only what's been reported to federal authorities. By other estimates, millions of people are victimized by identity theft each year and one study found that in 2014 alone, identity thieves cost consumers and business roughly $16 billion.

The list of banks, companies and organizations that maintain personal data on consumers is extensive; unfortunately, scores of them have had security breaches when hackers and other criminals stole sensitive customer data. According to the Identity Theft Resource Center, in the first eight months of 2016 alone, there were more than 630 data breaches in the U.S., nearly rivaling the 780 breaches recorded in all of 2015. CVS, Home Depot, JP Morgan Chase, Scottrade, Subway and Target have all suffered major data breaches. A 2016 HSB Cyber Survey showed that one in three Americans had been hacked over the past year.

At the corporate level, the problem has gotten so bad that lawmakers in some states are considering whether to impose stiff fines and penalties on retailers and other companies that don't take adequate precautions and wind up experiencing theft of client data. If your information is stolen from a bank, or you lose your credit card, the law limits your liability for credit card fraud to $50; however, if you report a lost card before it is used, you can avoid paying any amount at all.

Even the IRS has been hacked. In 2015, cyber thieves managed to swipe the social security numbers and other personal data of more than 700,000 U.S. taxpayers. In 2016, the IRS revealed that it was hacked yet again and another 101,000 people had their social security numbers stolen. What's worse: a security tool that the IRS had offered to tax fraud victims – a special PIN system – was also breached by identity thieves, forcing the IRS to suspend use of the tool.

Unfortunately, the IRS isn't alone. In 2015, a separate hack targeting the U.S. Office of Personnel Management exposed the personal information of 22 million current and former federal employees. So my point is: if federal agencies can't even protect sensitive data, you'd be foolish to rely exclusively on government entities, let alone businesses and others organizations, to handle this challenge alone. Instead, you have to arm yourself in this fight too. Fortunately, in the war against identity theft, there's plenty that you can – and should – do on your own.

at the job," says Linda Foley, executive director of the Identity Theft Resource Center. She highlights several areas of concern:

- Job applications that require Social Security numbers
- Timecards that mandate Social Security information and are stored in public areas
- Health insurance cards with Social Security numbers as the membership numbers
- Unlocked personnel file cabinets
- The absence of locking drawers in many cubicles

Compounding the problem, employees are often reluctant to report identity theft to their bosses. "Employers sometimes have an unwritten policy: 'Don't bring your personal problems to work.' So victims may not want to draw attention to themselves," says Linda Foley.

Scams Affect Both Workers and Those Looking For Work

Widespread layoffs across corporate America are also giving rise to another work-related identity theft con known as "the resume scam." In this swindle, con artists post fake job listings in newspapers or on the Internet. When you respond with a resume, they call or e-mail you and request more background information. But once they get your personal data, they disappear. Much later, you discover unauthorized credit purchases or newly opened accounts in your name.

Linda Foley says educating people about ways to protect themselves against this kind of deception is often "a double-edged sword."

"The minute we go public about a scam, while it helps to tell consumers what to avoid, it also gives ideas to criminals about what to do," she says.

Here are some ways to limit your chances of falling victim to identity theft on the job:

- Don't carry your Social Security card in your wallet
- Leave credit cards at home, unless absolutely necessary
- Ask your employer to keep personnel information in a secure environment
- Request a locking drawer or storage area for your personal items – and use it constantly. (Explain to your boss that you don't want to carry your purse, bag or briefcase with you each time you leave your desk to get coffee, go to the restroom, or attend a meeting)

Despite your own personal efforts, realize that it will take a change in business practices to stem the tide of workplace identity theft. Says Linda Foley: "The first line of defense in combating this problem always has been – and always will be – the business community. Because that's where the majority of information is collected, stored, and maintained."

Identity Theft Insurance

Many years ago, I used to think that identity theft insurance was unnecessary. But I changed my mind after seeing identity theft become such a widespread occurrence. So here's my advice: if you can afford it, identity theft coverage is certainly worth a look.

Numerous companies sell identity theft insurance. But the single best product on the market, in my opinion, is offered via LifeLock. Although no company can completely prevent identity theft, Lifelock's insurance is designed to quickly detect and immediately alert you to potential ID threats – and then resolve any issues you encounter.

So for starters, LifeLock's insurance can keep tabs on nearly all your personal data, such as your changes to your credit reports and scores; suspicious activity with your credit cards, checking, savings or investment accounts; and data breaches at institutions with whom you do business. If anything fishy happens – say, someone opens a credit card account in your name using a different address – LifeLock will give you a heads up about the matter. What I like most about LifeLock's offering, however, is that it doesn't solely monitor your information for suspected fraud, like most other companies do. Instead, LifeLock's ID theft coverage also fixes identity theft problems. LifeLock does this by providing you with 24-7 access to trained professionals experienced in dealing with ID theft cases. LifeLock will also pay up to $1 million to hire experts, lawyers and other specialists needed to clean up the havoc wrought by identity thieves.

Finally, LifeLock has always offered reimbursements to ID theft victims, to cover you for things like time lost on the job, travel expenses, and document replacement fees. But as of 2016, LifeLock's ID theft insurance now also includes a cash reimbursement element for those who lose money due to fraudulent withdrawals by crooks. Depending on which LifeLock policy you buy, you could be reimbursed up to $25,000, $100,000 or $1,000,000 in stolen funds replacement. LifeLock's standard insurance policy, which reimburses you $25,000 worth of stolen funds, currently costs $9.99 per month. LifeLock's mid-tier offering, called LifeLock Advantage, offers up to $100,000 in reimbursements for stolen funds, and costs $19.99 monthly. Meanwhile, LifeLock's deluxe identity theft insurance program, dubbed LifeLock Ultimate Plus, will reimburse you up to

$1,000,000 in stolen funds (from bank or investment accounts); this insurance costs $29.99 per month.

By comparison, if you check out www.myfico.com, you'll see that the cost of insurance for their deluxe security product (FICO Identity Ultimate) is $29.95 per month, with a 3-month minimum. It gives you weekly monitoring from over 400 data sources, email alerts when your personal information changes, provides you with access to your FICO Score and TransUnion credit report four times a year, and also supplies you with a $1 million identity theft insurance policy. It's a decent offering, but the benefits you get from LifeLock's program are far greater for pretty much the exact same price.

The Insurance Information Institute (III) also reports that a handful of insurance companies now offer identity theft protection. The insurance reimburses crime victims for the costs they incur in restoring their identity and repairing their credit reports – anything from lost wages to phone bills to, sometimes, attorneys' fees. The protection is sold as either part of a homeowner's policy, or as a stand-alone policy or an endorsement to a homeowner's or renter's insurance policy.

What to Do if Your Identity Is Stolen

Don't be shy about reaching out for help if your identity is stolen. Ignoring the problem won't make it go away. The sooner you act, the better. Report identity theft at once to the three major credit bureaus. They will put an "alert" on your credit file and you will be able to get a free copy of your credit report. Make a point to regularly check your credit file from now on. Sometimes identity thieves don't instantly go on shopping sprees – either because they're selling your information to others or because they're just laying low. In either case, you may not see any suspicious activity – like unauthorized charges or new accounts you didn't open – until months later. You should also immediately report identity theft to your local police department, and the Federal Trade Commission (www.ftc.gov or 877- ID-THEFT). For help and other resources, contact the Identity Theft Resource Center in San Diego at www.idtheftcenter.org or call 858-693- 7935.

Day 12: Set up a good filing system

One of the best things you can do to get financially fit in this year is to get yourself financially organized. So many of us want to whip our finances into shape, yet the task seems especially daunting because most households are overwhelmed by mounds of paperwork. But wouldn't it be great to have an easy, workable system for organizing all your financial documents like those numerous credit card receipts, old bills, tax records, and quarterly investment statements? Well, here are some tips from a few experts that will help you get a handle on all your paperwork, streamline your home or office, better balance your time, and enhance your records and document management skills. As of today you're going to create an easy-to-use filing and financial record-keeping system.

Being Organized Helps Your Finances

In case you need any motivation, first consider all the benefits of getting rid of piles upon piles of paperwork and creating, for example, a decent filing system for your financial records. In the book *Let Go of Clutter*, author Harriet Schechter says well-organized people can eliminate clutter and the stress related to it. They can also prevent piles of mail from accumulating, shed sentimental stuff without regret, and manage "mental clutter," she says.

Creating an Effective Filing System

To make an effective filing system, experts recommend alphabetizing your relevant documents by subject or category. But don't make the mistake of having too many or too few categories. A dozen broad categories should be the maximum in any filing system, Schechter says. Therefore, a sample file index might include categories for:

- Banking records (including checking and savings accounts)
- Bills paid (where you file regular monthly expenses)
- Budget (for itemized listings of all your expenses, income and assets)
- Credit cards (useful for storing receipts, statements and contracts)
- Insurance (auto, health, life and property insurance records)
- Investments (such as 401(k) and mutual fund reports)
- Mortgage
- Receipts
- Taxes

What to Keep – and What to Throw Away

Once you've gotten your files labeled, you may wonder how long you should keep certain financial documents. "As a rule, you should keep old tax records for at least seven years because that's how far back the law allows the IRS to go when it wants to audit you," says David Bach, a New York financial advisor and the author of *Smart Women Finish Rich*.

You should also hang on to your stock, bond and mutual fund statements indefinitely – mainly because if you sell any of those investments later, you may need to demonstrate the cost basis of your investment to the IRS. Bach notes, however, that you don't need to keep those prospectuses that mutual fund companies mail you each quarter, so you can safely toss those.

Additionally, Schechter says "when it doubt, throw it out," when it comes to things like magazine articles, seminar handouts and other "resource" materials you may have collected over the years.

How to Establish Adequate Backup Records

An important part of your record-keeping strategy in keeping solid financial records should be to make sure that you have backups of important documents. Remember hurricanes Katrina and Rita, and the devastation they caused throughout the Gulf Coast region of the United States? Not only were many lives lost, but more than 350,000 homes were significantly damaged or destroyed by these natural disasters, according to the Red Cross. Unfortunately, amid the ruins, many homeowners also lost critical financial documents, like wills, passports, and copies of life insurance policies. The same thing happened with more recent weather-related events, including hurricanes, tornadoes, fires and earthquakes of all kinds.

Here are five suggestions as to how you might back up your financial records. Feel free to try whatever options you feel most comfortable with, based on your particular circumstances.

1. Create a list of where everything is, from your account numbers to the physical location of all your important documents.
2. Use online software services like Backblaze, Carbonite, Memeo, and others. These programs automatically funnel copies of your data to a secure website that you can access when you need to access your data. Some services schedule backups, while others back your data up constantly during low-activity periods.
3. Scan such documents as marriage or birth certificates, copies of your homeowner's deed, or your most recent 1040 tax forms.

4. Get a USB flash drive or an external hard drive, and save your list of critical financial information onto that drive. Some come with encryption, so no one can read your sensitive information, like your credit card account numbers, without knowing your alphanumeric code.

5. Get a bank safe deposit box or use a safe at your home to store the USB flash drive/external hard drive. Alternatively, you can copy the information from your USB flash drive onto an additional drive, or put in on the hard drive of a trusted relative or friend.

6. Keep an "evacuation box," as suggested by The Financial Planning Association. This is a box that is fireproof, contains a lock, and is light enough to tote away in the event of an emergency.

Maintaining Your Filing System

Once you've got a working system, the final step is to stay on top of your paperwork, so that it doesn't spiral out of control. Resist the urge to have general mail files – like the dreaded, all-purpose "in" and "out" baskets that seem to occupy almost every home office and work desk space. Instead, create a paper-flow system that instantly tells you what you're supposed to do with the mail that's held there. For example, to quickly sort through mail – and it's best to do that the same day that it arrives – you can put it into categories labeled:

- "To Pay" (for bills, charitable solicitations, etc.)
- "To Read,"
- "To File,"
- "Correspondence,"

- "Pending/Follow-ups,"
- "Events/Invitations," or
- "To Share/Forward."

Once you weed through your files, purging unnecessary paperwork and reducing the amount of piles you have stacked up, chances are you'll be a lot clearer about your finances – and certainly better organized. What's more, if you take a few minutes each day to tackle your paperwork, you'll save yourself many hours – if not days – of having to wade through a morass of papers later in the year when you're trying to find some important document. This is particularly true when tax time rolls around. Imagine how great it would feel if you didn't have to go sifting through old piles of paper trying to justify all your tax deductions. Instead, you could simply turn over to your accountant or to a paid tax professional a nice, neat file of well-organized receipts and records. I can't guarantee you that you'll be paying Zero Taxes ... but I can promise you that having organized paperwork, and a well-kept filing system is a strategy that will make tax time a lot less taxing!

Day 13: Face the truth about your situation

Is your financial house in excellent, good, fair, poor or dire condition? Often, circumstances beyond our control or unexpected life events, such as divorce, job loss or a death in the family can ruin one's finances. But in this chapter, I want you to consider also all the things you have done – both positive and negative – that have put your financial house in its present state.

Your Finances & the Laws of Cause and Effect

As a Money Coach, I teach a workshop called "Get Financially Fit Now!" One lesson that I tell participants is:

> *Your current financial situation is directly tied to your own actions (or lack thereof), because your finances operate according to the laws of "cause and effect."*

What this means is that we have to first look in the mirror and determine what financial mistakes we have been making and what actions we might have taken to cause or continue our financial troubles. In some cases, it may not have been what we've done, but what we've procrastinated about, or failed to do, that has led to financial difficulties.

Again, there are certainly events that happen – such as illnesses or accidents – that are no fault of our own. But what I'm talking about are the financial problems we face that can be directly attributed to actions we have taken, or have neglected to take. Let's stop talking money for a minute and look beyond the economic world. Instead, let's examine other areas of life: the physical, natural and mechanical realms. Each area illustrates the laws of "cause and effect."

Physical Realm

When obesity occurs, frequently it is caused by improper nutrition and a lack of exercise. Barring some medical condition that causes one to gain weight, doctors agree that they best way to restore oneself to a proper weight and good health is to eat right and exercise regularly. If you fail to do this, obesity results.

Natural Realm

You don't need a green thumb to know that dying plants or a weed-filled garden are often caused by lack of water, insufficient sunlight, or inadequate pruning. To get that garden back in good condition, you must tend to it and give it proper care.

Mechanical Realm

The reason auto manufacturers suggest you change your car's oil every 3,000 miles is because a lack of maintenance or excessive wear and tear will cause your vehicle to break down. You get regular checks at the doctor right? Well, using the same logic, your car should also get regular checkups at the mechanic.

In What Condition Is Your Financial House?

Whenever something is neglected or abused – no matter whether it's your body, your garden or your car – that thing will suffer. And the first order of business to get into good condition is to apply some care and attention.

The same principle holds true in the economic realm. When you neglect or abuse your financial house, the result is that it is in disrepair. And it won't get into tip-top condition until you start taking positive steps and stop doing the things that are detrimental to your financial condition.

So, here's your next action item: Make a list of what you have done right, and where you have clearly gone astray in conducting your personal financial affairs. Evaluate your past behavior as far as handling credit, paying bills on time, and managing your money. Whatever your present circumstances, I'd like for you to also think about how long your situation has been this way. Has it been less than a year, more than a year, two to five years, five to 10 years, or as long as you can remember?

Take 10 minutes or so and fill in the worksheet on the following page. It will guide you in your thinking and help you to face the truth about your current situation.

My Financial House

Instructions: Fill in the blanks with the correct statements.

My financial house is in _____ condition.

(excellent, good, fair, poor, or dire)

It has been that way for: _____

(Less than a year, more than a year, 2 to 5 years, 5 to 10 years, or as long as I can remember)

These are the things, good or bad, that I have done to put my financial house in its current state:

1. _____
2. _____
3. _____
4. _____
5. _____

These are the things I have neglected, or failed to do, that have resulted in my current financial condition:

1. _____
2. _____
3. _____
4. _____
5. _____

Your Financially Fit Check-up

Now I want you to take a quiz. It's a short, 10-question, true or false quiz. I call it the "Financially Fit Check-up."

I also give this quiz at seminars and workshops across the country – to investors who have a million dollars in net worth or better, and to unemployed people who are having trouble putting food on the table.

Don't be scared by the prospect of taking this little test. This quiz is just a snapshot of where you are today. It's meant to see how "Financially Fit" you are by examining the extent to which you've handled some financial matters in your life.

It's not intended to be a comprehensive look at your finances, nor is it meant to predict where you'll be, say, a year from now. It's simply designed to help give you a look at how things are – right here and now.

After you take the quiz, view the "Financially Fit Score Guide" on the following page, then "grade" your quiz. Two requests: first, don't cheat yourself! Answer the questions honestly. Also, don't look ahead to the score guide, just yet. Read it after you've actually taken the Financially Fit Quiz.

Financially Fit Check-Up

Please read the following 10 statements. Answer "True" or "false" as appropriate for you.

		T	F
1.	I have enough money to buy, do or achieve the things I want.	____	____
2.	I know exactly how much debt I owe and how much it costs me each month/year in interest.	____	____
3.	I never worry about bills.	____	____
4.	I feel financially secure.	____	____
5.	I have a written financial plan.	____	____
6.	I have an updated will.	____	____
7.	I know that I have adequate life and disability insurance.	____	____
8.	I have an emergency cash cushion of at least 3 months' expenses.	____	____
9.	I have a very clear idea about where my money goes each month.	____	____
10.	I feel confident about my money-management knowledge/skills.	____	____

Financially Fit Score Guide

DIRECTIONS: Give yourself 1 point for each "true" answer and 0 for each "false" answer. Add and enter your score here _____

8-10 Points: You have an extremely high degree of financial security and well- being. You are very **"Financially Fit."**

5-7 Points: You are on the right path to becoming **"Financially Fit."** You have made some wise choices and could benefit from making additional smart money moves.

2-4 Points: You are a good candidate to take some major steps to get **"Financially Fit."**

0-1 Point: Your financial health is in serious jeopardy. You need to immediately develop a plan and take action to get out of the economic Intensive Care Unit and into the **"Financially Fit"** Recovery Room.

How Does Your Score Compare to Others?

I've given this quiz to many thousands of people nationwide. And in case you are fretting over your score, let me tell you that roughly 70% of all the individuals who take this quiz score between 0 and 3.

I once gave a presentation at Rutgers University in Princeton, New Jersey where 2,000 people attended my seminar. In that crowd of 2,000, the highest score was a 7. Only one person – a 72-year-old retiree from Long Island named Maria – has ever scored a perfect 10. That says a lot about the state of most Americans' personal finances. You don't have to score a perfect 10 in order to be "Financially Fit." But you should certainly aim for a score of at least 6 or 7. If you follow the advice contained throughout *Zero Debt*, you can definitely do that – at a minimum.

Now that you've examined your financial house, and reflected on what you may have done (or not done) to cause your current situation, I want you to write out three things you're going to quickly do to improve your finances.

Here's what I'm going to do about it ...
In 24 hours, I will: _____
Within one week, I will: _____
Within one month, I will: _____

After you follow through on any one of your action items, write me at info@askthemoneycoach.com to tell me about your progress.

Day 14: Create SMART financial goals.

SMART is an abbreviation for goals that are Specific, Measurable, Action- Oriented, Realistic, and Time-Bound. The idea is to avoid general, vague or hazy goals such "I want to be rich." Exactly what does rich mean to you? Is it having $100,000, or $1 million in the bank? Also, what's your timetable and/or deadline?

The Importance of Written Goals

You must have precise, written goals – *not ideas in your head*. If you can't come up with your own written goals and the plan that will get you there, find a local financial planner for help. You can contact one in your area through the Financial Planning Association at 800-647-6340 or www.plannersearch.org. Another place to find a fee-only financial advisor is the National Association of Personal Financial Advisors at www.napfa.org or 800-366-2732. Finally, many accountants also offer financial planning services. To find one, contact the American Institute of Certified Public Accountants: www.aicpa.org or 212-596-6200.

In my first book, *Investing Success: How to Conquer 30 Costly Mistakes & Multiply Your Wealth!* I told readers about the importance of having SMART goals. I also explained that people who set written goals overwhelmingly fare better than those who do not. Put yourself with the first group – among those with written goals – if you want to get ahead financially.

Consider Your Short, Medium and Long-Range Goals

I'd like to guide your thinking now toward short-term, medium-range, and long-term goals that you may want to pursue. Short-term goals are those you can accomplish in one or two years at most. Medium-range goals will take two to 10 years to achieve. And long-term goals require you to save or invest for a decade or longer. Here are some goals to which you might aspire:

- Paying off student loans
- Eliminating credit card debt
- Building up an emergency cash cushion
- Buying a new car or a second automobile
- Starting a business
- Saving for a down-payment on a house
- Investing in the stock market or in real estate
- Retiring comfortably

Your Retirement Aspirations

Financial advisors say one of the most frequently asked questions from their clients is: Am I financially prepared for retirement? Yet far fewer people take time to ponder another, equally pressing query: Am I *emotionally* ready to retire?

Certainly, leaving the full-time workforce has serious financial implications. But too often, experts say, economic issues overshadow important emotional considerations.

So if you're planning for your Golden Years, do take time to enhance your retirement I.Q. – ensuring, among other things, that you'll have a healthy-sized nest egg.

But before you retire, don't forget to boost your retirement E.Q. (Emotional Quotient) as well. To ease into retirement with a lot more peace of mind, consider these three questions now – before you bid Corporate America or your current job farewell.

- **Where do you plan to live?**

If you still have a mortgage, or if you plan to purchase another home, this is clearly a financial issue – especially since housing prices vary widely nationwide. But where you will live during retirement is also an emotionally- laden topic, particularly for couples. Oftentimes, one partner may envision selling the house, moving out of state, or relocating to a warm climate. Meanwhile, the other partner may be sentimentally attached to the family home, may be wary of leaving the current neighborhood, or – far from desiring tropical weather – may want to move closer to the grandchildren in Minneapolis or Buffalo. Thus, talking beforehand with your spouse about these potential areas of disagreement can go a long way toward avoiding future conflicts. You don't want to tarnish your retirement together by being bitter over something as basic as where the two of you live, so address this issue early on.

- **How will you spend your time?**

Figuring out what do with the rest of your life will require some serious soul-searching. It's also important to debunk some myths about what retirement represents.

"A lot of people are afraid of what their lives will be like," says Jerry Kleiman, a clinical psychologist in Long Island, NY. "They associate retirement with diminished capacity, diminished usefulness in society, dependency, or being a step closer to death."

As a result, many people simply stop working and then ask "O.K. now what?"

Kleiman, who is also co-founder of Optimal Resolutions Inc., a consultancy that aids individuals and families with the emotional issues surrounding retirement, suggests that pre-retirees take a "life inventory." This requires you to identify unfulfilled dreams or goals, examine the hobbies and activities that excite you most, and determine what you are passionate about, in terms of intellectual, physical, social or spiritual pursuits.

Similarly, it's also crucial to realize what you don't want to do.

"I know some people who want to retire on a beach, and sit around and play cards all day. If I did that, I'd be dead within a year from boredom," says Mark Wachs, a publicist in New York. Wachs, who was 60 at the time I interviewed him, has been meeting with his financial planner recently to prepare for his retirement – a period he views as "the next phase" in his life.

- **If your finances fall short of your expectations, can you cope with that reality?**

Many of us have grown up with grandiose images of what retirement will be like: freedom from the stresses of work, time to travel, care-free days spent playing golf, or even doing absolutely nothing at all. Unfortunately, these images are more fiction than fact. The average American is woefully unprepared for the financial challenges of life without a steady paycheck – and thus unprepared to deal with the emotional letdown that inevitably occurs when retirement dreams and goals aren't realized.

One big shock for many people is that they probably won't be retiring at all – at least not as soon as, or in the manner, they'd hoped. Many financial experts predict a lot more retirees will continue to work part-time. Others will be forced to adopt a less expensive lifestyle.

With the stock market always gyrating so much, many people's original retirement plans may have to be postponed, or have only begun to recover. The financial crisis and credit crunch that wreaked havoc all across the globe meant it's more important than ever to manage debt wisely, particularly if you're approaching retirement.

Retirees and Debt

Unfortunately, more and more retirees are falling into debt at the exact point in their lives when they should be free from financial worries. Americans 65 and older carry an average of nearly $5,000 in credit card debt, according to Demos, a New York-based research and think tank. Part of this rising tide of debt is due to surging housing, healthcare and energy costs.

By getting your debts under control now, you can avoid that postponed or "delayed" retirement scenario – and ease into your Golden Years with Zero Debt and maximum financial freedom.

Week 3 Overview

This week, you will:

- √ Figure out where you will get money to pay off debt
- √ Scrutinize your spending
- √ Make a realistic budget
- √ Find 10 ways to cut your spending
- √ Adopt 5 lifestyle changes to save money
- √ Adjust your W4 withholdings if you get a refund
- √ Sell or donate stuff you don't need or want

Day 15: Figure out the $69,000 question: Where will you get the money to pay for your goals, such as slashing your debt?

There are many potential sources of funds you can tap in order to pay down your debts or fund other goals.

Below is a list of possible cash sources. Next to each of these items, write one of the following letter codes, based on your chances of getting cash from each source:

Write **V** for "Very Likely"; **P** for "Possible"; **NL** for "Not Likely"; and **I** for "Impossible".

- Salary/Wages   _____
- Self-Employment Income   _____
- Tips   _____
- Second Job   _____
- Inheritance/Gifts   _____
- Borrowed Money (i.e. bank or family) _____
- Alimony   _____
- Pension   _____
- Social Security   _____
- Savings   _____
- Investments   _____
- Sell Goods Owned (car, furniture, etc.) _____

This is a practical look at your options. Start to consider your circumstances realistically, and think about if you have any other unique sources of funding that you might tap.

Day 16: Scrutinize your spending.

As mentioned before, the average U.S. household spends $1.22 for every $1 it earns, according to research from Northwestern Mutual. That's a recipe for a lifetime of debt. Yet, many of us spend well beyond our means. This is an area I know about all too well, because for many years I was a very big spender. That's a part of my life and personality that I have to carefully manage, even now.

How I Got Out of $100,000 in Credit Card Debt

I count myself very fortunate. I once had just over $100,000 in credit card debt, and now I have Zero Debt. When I say I have Zero Debt, I should clarify that: I no longer have any credit card bills – the worst form of "bad" debt. I still have a mortgage. Fortunately, I've managed to pay off the loans I had from undergraduate and graduate school. All were at interest rates below 6%. Mortgage debt and college financing are often described as "good" debt. A home is the foundation for wealth building and can be leveraged for investment purposes. Debt associated with your home has tax advantages, as well. My graduate school education at the University of Southern California – even the loans that financed my Master of Arts degree from USC – represented an investment in my future. Having an advanced degree has afforded me greater earnings over the years.

With regard to my $100,000-plus credit card debt, though, I am pleased to say that I have paid off everything I owed to creditors. What may be even more startling to most people is that I paid my debts without credit counseling, without enrolling in any debt management program, and without resorting to bankruptcy. What I did do was educate myself, read the fine print on my agreements, and get smart about my use of credit. I was also lucky, very lucky, that I didn't get a single negative mark on my credit file even when I had so much debt.

Ultimately, I paid what I owed – in full and with interest. The interest I shelled out – many thousands of dollars – was the price I paid for overspending and racking up debt, year after year.

Being In Debt Denial

When I reflect on my debt, I realize now I was very much in denial. I definitely had a debt problem for years. But I was one of those people who would never admit it. After all, I was a financial journalist. I knew a lot about making money, saving it, and investing it. In fact, I was doing a lot of the right things economically – like socking away pre-tax earnings in my 401(k) every year, putting aside money for my kids' college education, protecting my family with life insurance, and so on. To top it off, I had a nice six-figure salary. So in my head, the fact that I'd amassed this huge $100,000 in debt was somehow okay. Of course, I know now that it was anything but okay.

I ran up large amounts of debts in several ways. First, I made poor choices with my money, mainly in that my family lived a lifestyle that, in truth, exceeded our income level at the time. We traveled whenever we wanted to, frequently bought gifts and gave money to people, paid for an expensive private school for my children, purchased any kind of electronics or gadgets we wanted, and so forth. I rationalized that the things I was buying were the things my family *needed*. The reality is that it was mainly just stuff we *wanted*.

Living beyond our means caused us to also use credit to pay for our normal monthly bills from time to time. But a big chunk of my credit card debt came, believe it or not, from a single big-ticket purchase. In 2001, I bought two plots of land for $37,500 at a city auction. My plan was to quickly build a few multi-family homes on the land, sell the properties and net $150,000 bucks. To acquire the land quickly, I didn't bother with getting bank financing or a construction loan. Instead, I just got cash advances from my credit cards and those handy checks that credit card companies sent me, month after month. I figured any financing charges I paid would ultimately be worth it. I even convinced myself that I "owned" the land outright – simply because no bank held a mortgage on the property. Well, it's true that I was the owner, on paper, but it was the credit cards that really financed the purchase.

To make a long story short, the "quick" real estate deal I envisioned never happened. But the debt remained. To get rid of it, I started negotiating for lower interest rates, paying aggressively on my credit card bills and immediately turning over to my creditors any "extra" money I received.

Downsizing Hits Home

In early 2003, I lost my six-figure television job as a *Wall Street Journal* reporter for CNBC. Like millions of others in corporate America, I, too, was laid off in a cost-cutting move. (Remember the five Dreaded D's – Downsizing, Death, Divorce, Disability and Disease – that I told you could throw your finances awry or exacerbate existing problems?)

Even after my layoff, I didn't rein in my spending. In fact, my spending increased dramatically because I launched my own business and spent about $100,000 funding it in 2003 and early 2004. This time, though, I primarily used my savings. But even amid my downsizing, I didn't go deeper in debt. From 2001 to 2004, I'd spent three years managing that debt, negotiating with creditors and paying big chunks of money to drastically reduce about $70,000 worth of credit card bills. I did everything I could think of to whittle away my debts, including many of the strategies outlined on this book: I cut back on spending, I overhauled my budget, I used windfalls like tax refund checks to knock out credit card bills, I negotiated to get lower interest rates, I did balance transfers to get 0% deals on my credit card, I tripled my credit card payments, and more. It wasn't until early 2004 that I finally paid off the last $30,000 of all my debts in full thanks to – can you guess? – that real estate investment I made back in 2001. Turns out buying the land was a smart investment, after all, just not in a way that I'd ever imagined. I never built a thing on it. But the land alone shot up in value and I received $200,000 for it from a cash buyer – more than five times what I paid for it.

So, yes, I'm a Zero Debt convert now, a zealot you might say. But to get here, I've paid a high price for over-spending and for racking up large amounts of debts in the past. For instance, because I wasn't really adding to my debts in 2003 and 2004, I tapped other forms of available funds – and in my case it was hard-earned savings. I took $80,000, for example, out of my 401(k) plan – a money mistake I'd never advise anyone else to make.

Don't Be Ashamed of Mistakes – Just Fix Them

I tell you my story in the hopes that you won't be ashamed of the money mistakes you've made. I also want you to know that you're not alone in your debt woes, and that no matter how bad it seems, there is always a way out.

I also reveal my story because I want you to take an honest look at your own spending patterns. The financial seminars I conduct, along with my coaching programs and online financial boot camps, are designed to help people jumpstart their finances and learn to manage their money. In workshops and one-on-one coaching, I often ask people to distinguish between things that are "luxuries" and things that are "necessities." Invariably, one person will cite some thing – be it a good or a service – as a "necessity" that another person believes is a "luxury."

I then encourage people to gain some perspective on their spending by considering those things that, to them, may seem like necessities, but that to others appear more like luxuries, or even frivolous or downright wasteful spending.

For example, I once told a group of workshop participants that I spent about $300 a month on books. Some attendees were mortified! They gave me all kinds of suggestions (good ones, in fact), about how I could definitely save money by checking out books from the library, reading books in the bookstore, or sharing books with friends, etc. Most people clearly saw my monthly book-buying binge as a luxury – if not a wasteful use of my money – whereas I saw it as a "necessity."

As it so happens, I'm a big believer in the power of books, education and learning from others. I also know that the average millionaire tends to be (like I am) a voracious reader, devouring anywhere from two to six books per month. So spending what is admittedly a small fortune on books didn't strike me as particularly harmful or unnecessary. On the contrary, I saw it as a necessary part of my self-education and self-improvement. Nonetheless, I did take people's advice! While I've kept feeding my book habit over the years, I just do it smarter now; I spend less money on books, but I'm still an avid reader.

You'd be surprised at how others might see your spending habits. And because I think some outside perspective can be a big eye-opener, I'd like you to take a moment to do the following exercise.

Gaining Perspective on Your Spending

What's a luxury? What is frivolous? What is wasteful?

Directions: Take a few moments by yourself to complete the following statements, filling in the appropriate information. Think about things you spend money on that you consider "necessities," but that outsiders might not view that way.

I now spend $_____ weekly/monthly/yearly on _____ something some people may consider a luxury.

I also spend $_____ weekly/monthly/yearly on _____ which other people might view as frivolous.

Furthermore, I spend $_____ a week/month/year on _____ which certain people could think is wasteful.

Now go ask a family member or friend to read aloud your statements. Then ask him/her to honestly answer 3 questions:

1. Do you think any of the things I am spending money on are "luxuries," "frivolous," or "wasteful?"
2. Why or why not?
3. Is there a better way for me to eliminate or reduce these expenses?

After you receive some feedback, put one or two recommendations from relatives or friends into practice if they make sense and if the advice will save you money.

Day 17: Make a *realistic* budget.

If you've read this far into *Zero Debt*, I have to assume that you're not just a casual reader – you've likely had your fair share of money woes. Well, I'm a firm believer that when most people experience cash-flow problems with their budgets, it's usually caused by one of two things:

Causes of Cash Flow Problems

1) You *Don't* Have A Budget ... Or
2) You *Do* Have A Budget ... *But* ...

It gets blown by that dirty, rotten **S.C.U.M.**

What is SCUM? Let me tell you right away that it's not: "Some Cousin, Uncle or Mama" – although you may feel like certain relatives are draining you financially! SCUM actually stands for "Something Came Up Monthly."

How many times have you thought you were getting ahead on your bills, only to have something "come up" that you didn't anticipate? It could be that you loan money to a friend in need; someone in the family gets sick; your kid's school has a fund-raising drive – whatever. The end result is always the same: some unexpected expense fouls up your budget.

Now for some people, the real problem is that they've never truly created a written budget at all. They just spend willy-nilly and hope that checks don't bounce.

But even those people who actually do make plans seem to constantly blow their budgets. In the blanks below, fill in some expenses that you believe may rear their ugly heads when you least "expect" them to:

S _____

C _____

U _____

M _____

4 Simple Steps to Stop Blowing Your Budget

In fact, each month, millions of Americans dutifully plan their household budgets – only to have some unforeseen event come along and totally wreck what are seemingly well-made financial plans.

If you ask most of these people how their budgets went awry, the response will almost invariably be: "Something came up," followed by an explanation about how their house roof leaked, their car conked out, or someone in the family unexpectedly took ill.

While unanticipated situations can certainly spoil even the best-laid economic plans, why is it that many individuals blow their budgets month after month after month? In my many years of talking to consumers, financial counselors and money management experts, I've come to the conclusion that true "emergencies" – like those described above – actually happen relatively infrequently. So while most people *think* they run out of money because some emergency "came up," the reality is that most people blow their budgets because **LIFE** happened to them.

LIFE is an acronym that describes the four ways that your budget gets out of whack – forcing you to spend more than you planned for the month, or causing you to live from paycheck to paycheck.

- **Listed items are under-calculated.**

  The "L" in LIFE stands for expenses that are "Listed" items in your budget, but your numbers are actually way off the mark. Unfortunately, many individuals who draw up budgets don't use very precise numbers. People have a tendency to underestimate their spending. Take cellular phones, for example. If you own one, you probably account for it in your monthly budget with a figure like $49.99 – or whatever your basic monthly charge happens to be. But do you find that you regularly talk beyond your allotted cell phone minutes/data plan, so that you wind up with a mobile phone bill closer to $80 per month? If so, you need to adjust your budget and put in more realistic numbers for this expense. Household bills, like electricity and gas, are another area where people get tripped up. They include these expenses as a flat cost in their budgets, say $100 a month. But their heating or air conditioning bill is routinely far more than that $100, especially during times of extreme weather.

- **Impulse purchases seduce you.**

  We all make impulse purchases from time to time – but some people do it on a regular basis. It may be that you're reading the newspaper and you see a discount coupon for a retail store you like. And before long, you're at the mall, shopping. Other times, you may be surfing the Internet looking for information, when a pop-up seduces you with some intriguing advertisement. Next thing you know, you've whipped out your credit card to buy some product or service.

- **Forgotten bills surface.**

  Some bills get paid annually or perhaps twice a year. If you're not careful in your planning, you can exclude these expenses from your budget, and then, when the bills come due, you realize you forgot all about them. Has this ever happened to you? If so, don't omit from your budget those expenditures that may not be paid on a monthly basis – things like your homeowner's or auto insurance, the maintenance fee for the vacation timeshare you own, your gym membership, or any annual fees you pay to belong to personal, professional or civic organizations.

- **Emergency or unexpected events occur.**

  Last, there are obviously times when emergencies – like a burst boiler unit – can ruin a budget. Try to minimize these events with preventative measures, such as regularly servicing your boiler, having routine maintenance done on your car to avoid breakdowns, and making periodic visits to the doctor to stave off serious medical conditions.

  Once you realize that **LIFE** happens to everyone, you can take some steps to safeguard your budget. Start by reviewing your finances and taking a hard, realistic look at your overall spending habits. If you've been vastly under-calculating listed items in your budget, make the necessary adjustments. If you make too many impulse purchases, carry less cash with you or put your credit cards away, to minimize the temptation to buy on a whim. Fine-tune your budget so you don't forget any one-off bills. Also, consider what you can do to reduce those "emergency" situations – especially the kind that can be cured with a little preventive medicine. Finally, think very hard about your own budget busters.

Listed items were under-calculated

Impulse buying

Forgotten bills

Emergencies or unexpected expenses

Now list some of your budget busters below. Place a letter – L, I, F, or E – next to each one. Do you see any patterns? What are your budget busters?

What are your budget busters?

L   I   F   E

1. _____ ☐

2. _____ ☐

3. _____ ☐

4. _____ ☐

Day 18: Find 10 ways to cut your spending.

Today I want you to come up with 10 ways to cut your spending. Don't complain about it or say it's impossible. Just put your thinking cap on and get busy. If you really had to – and at this point, you do really have to in order to eliminate your money problems – I'm sure you could be really creative.

But just to jumpstart your thinking, I'll start you out with 10 ideas:

- Do your own home maintenance
- Only go to your bank's ATMs
- Bring lunch to work daily or a few days a week
- Visit www.creditcardperks.com for a lower credit card rate
- Stop smoking (or drinking)
- Carpool
- Use coupons (always or from time to time)
- Buy in bulk
- Raise your insurance deductibles
- Plan and pay for travel in advance

Saving Money Doesn't Have To Be a Big Hassle

I'm constantly amazed at how many people pay full price for products and services – when they could so readily get the things they need for a lot less money.

For many consumers, though, the idea of saving big bucks on everything from soap and toilet paper to a new car or medical insurance means either hours of coupon clipping and haggling with salesmen. Neither tactic is especially attractive for busy people who have family, career and other demands on their time.

Thankfully, there are some fast, painless and – dare I say it? – fun ways to save money, simply by hopping on the Internet. After all, who doesn't relish snagging a true bargain?

Take your homeowner's or auto insurance. To save money there, check out www.insure.com. They comparison shop for you and get you the best insurance rates. Since homeowner's coverage averages $1,034 a year, according to the latest figures from the National Association of Insurance Commissioners (NAIC), and auto insurance another $841, (according to the Insurance Information Institute) if you spend 20 minutes surfing the web to save 10% on these insurance expenses, you can easily put nearly $200 back into your bank account.

And don't forget to look for ways to curb costs on big-ticket items, such as your mortgage or car note. If you want to slash the amount of money you're doling out for your monthly car payment, it is well worth it to visit www.capitalone.com. They let you refinance your existing auto loan. Typical time it takes to fill out the application: 10 to 15 minutes. Average savings: $700 per year.

If you're a person who gets into a grocery or clothing store and loses your mind, buying indiscriminately and not getting a lot of value for your hard-earned money, get some help from the experts at sites like www.thesimpledollar.com or www.mrmoneymustache.com. These sites give you great tips on how to save money on a variety of products and services using tried and true strategies that work.

Day 19: Adopt five lifestyle changes to save more money

Have you ever thought about how making small changes in the way to live can actually save you loads of money? Well, today I'd like you to think about your lifestyle and what areas might be out of whack with your current desires to become financially free – and achieve Zero Debt status.

For example, do you live in a metropolitan area and take cabs too frequently – instead of hopping aboard the less expensive subway or rail system?

Do you entertain once a month or more at your home – I'm not talking lavish parties, but certainly large enough or frequent enough shindigs (or even pizza and beer bashes!) that you have to dole out a lot of money for food and drinks, etc.?

Do you think you're "above" wearing clothes that don't carry a designer label?

Maybe none of these situations describes your lifestyle. That's fine. I still want you to think about how it is that you're living.

We all have areas of our life where, with minor adjustments, we can save money. My goal here isn't to send you into "can't have" or "can't do" mode. I simply want you to consider less-expensive options, or alternatives to what you may be currently doing.

Again, to get you going, here are five lifestyle changes from which I think most people could benefit:

When shopping, never pay full retail price

That's right. I said NEVER pay full retail. You might be thinking, *"How is that even possible?"* Well, for starters, you can wait for the item to go on sale, you could find equivalent bargains online, you might also hit outlets or discount stores, or you can simply say: "I don't need/want it that badly" – and walk away. (For those of you with a shopping Jones, please read the special advice at the end of this chapter called "How to Look like a Million Bucks without Spending a Fortune.")

Become a frequent library patron

Borrow videos/DVDs and books, instead of purchasing them. The average new release video or DVD now costs anywhere from $15 to $30 (depending on if you get it on sale). Even if you buy just 10 a year, making the switch to borrowed videos/DVDs will save you hundreds of dollars. If your households buys dozens of videos or DVDs annually (and many families do have hundreds of videos/ DVDs in their collections), you'll save thousands. Alternatively, get a low cost Netflix subscription to watch movies. You'll come out much better.

Take advantage of free/low-cost attractions/events in your city

Enjoy parades, museums, and city parks rather than expensive outings like amusement parks. Most are free of charge, including museums, which offer free admission on certain days of the week/ month.

Eat out less often

Saving $5 a day by skipping fast food or restaurants will keep $1,825 a year in your pocket; $10 a day means an annual savings of $3,650.

Walk, versus driving, to any place in walking distance

You'll save money on gas, help the environment, and be healthier too!

My point is that there are probably some behavioral patterns in your life – some things that you do frequently, buy regularly or spend money on all the time – that may not be financially feasible or prudent at this time. If so, see if you can change those things. And who knows: After a few months, you might even find that you *enjoy* the lifestyle adjustments. One thing is certain: you'll have a fatter bank account to show for your actions.

On the following pages, you'll find a special chapter supplement for all you serious shopaholics out there – guys and gals! This information was included in my first book, *Investing Success*, because I realize there are so many people out there who feel financially pinched because of their spending habits. So if you've got too many bills to pay, and a little less cash than you'd like to go around, try the following ideas. They represent my Top 10 Rules for Money-Wise Shoppers.

Look Like a Million Bucks without Spending a Fortune

1. **Never pay full retail price. Ever**

   I'm not suggesting that you walk into Barney's, or even your local department store, and start haggling over prices. But any savvy fashion editor or stylist will tell you that nobody (in the know) pays the full asking price for anything these days. Here are a few pointers:

   - For starters, you can ***wait until the item goes on sale*** (trust me, it will!)
   - ***Shop sample sales*** in major cities and get designer duds for

a fraction of the retail price. These to-die-for sales usually happen after Fashion Week in New York, Los Angeles, London, Milan and Paris

- *Buy classic styles off-season.* Great pieces look good season to season.
- *Hop online.* All of these websites sell designer merchandise both in an off-season:
  - **decadesinc.com** (for vintage chic);
  - **yoox.com**, (for Italian designers);
  - **bluefly.com** (for designer clothing);
  - **ebay.com** (yes, ebay! It offers high-end designer clothes, including some that hit the Net before they're available nationally)

- *Think Outlets, Outlets, Outlets.* Outlet malls and factory stores can help you score great money-saving deals. But the trick is to know how and why you're getting a screaming bargain. For instance, are those leather jackets 80% off because the manufacturer made far too many and shipped the overruns to the outlet store? Or is that ultra low price tag a result of those jackets being irregular items – with funky stitching or one sleeve shorter than the other?

- Finally, *you can actually negotiate* in many boutiques and specialty stores. Don't be obnoxious about it. But when you find something you want, just sort of wrinkle your nose up a bit and, while holding the price tag, ever-so-nicely ask the sales person: "*$75? Is that the best price you can offer me?*"

2. **Don't shop another day until you organize your closet.**

In your head, you may think you need another black skirt. But you probably just *want* one, because if you carefully go through your closet (that's right, sort out all those folded piles and even the stuff in bags and tucked away in the corners), you'll probably find that you have at least two or three – and likely even more – perfectly fine black skirts. So it's hard to justify buying yet another black skirt under these circumstances. By organizing your closet, you'll also be far less prone to making impulse purchases of other things you mistakenly believe you "need."

3. **Think like a celebrity**

When you see Halle Berry or Jennifer Lopez donning a gorgeous dress, wearing Harry Winston jewels or even sporting a sexy pair of Jimmy Choo shoes, *realize that they rarely pay for these clothes and accessories.* In fact, designers shower them with goods knowing that having these A- list celebrities wear their clothes will be good publicity, and thus boost sales. The celebs themselves more often than not will wear the item once (if the designer is lucky). But then that item gets donated to charity or tossed in the back of what I'm sure is the world's largest walk-in closet. In any event, consider this: Since multi-millionaire "superstars" aren't even paying to look like stars, why should you? If you keep in mind that a $1,000 dress you're pining away for is probably only realistically going to be worn by you just once (like the stars do), chances are you may be willing to forego splurging on that item, if you can't really afford it.

4. **Take a friend shopping.**

   And I don't mean your girlfriend whose Visa bill is constantly more than her rent. I'm talking about your level-headed friend, the one who doesn't call you every other week to borrow money because her paycheck has run out. One suggestion though: don't drag along a pal (however well- intentioned) who simply can't have fun on your shopping quest. Instead, bring along your "I-know-how-to-enjoy-myself-too-but-I'm-not-going- to-squander-my-rent-payment-to-do-it" buddy. What's the point of all this? A friend with a good head on her shoulders will keep you from making outlandish purchases and wasting your money. She'll make you accountable for your spending actions. And accountability counts.

5. **Establish a pre-set limit before you go shopping.**

   Just come up with a ballpark figure (say $300) and let that serve as your cap. Now here's where you get to enjoy yourself – and not feel deprived. Mentally allow yourself the option of going 10% over your pre-set limit. So if you absolutely CAN'T do without a $50 bra and panties set, but you've already reached your $300 limit, you can go ahead and make the purchase, and do so guilt-free. Any spending beyond that, though, and you're asking for trouble. This way, if you stick to your pre-set limit, you'll be patting yourself on the back. If you go as high as your spending-cap- plus-10% limit, at least you've still stayed within the guidelines, without breaking the bank. Bonus: if you actually spend 10% under, celebrate! One caveat: don't spend the 10% you saved (and then some) on an expensive dinner or some other one-time event. Instead, sock that money away into a "hands-off" savings account.

6. **Go where the real bargains are**

Serious fashionistas who can swing it go to London or Milan for fashion bargains. The cost of the airplane ticket can be well worth it if you pick up, say, Italian boots for $100 that you'd spend $450 for in the U.S. This tip isn't to suggest that you go into debt – or that you take a trip you can't afford, just for clothes. You'd obviously only use this strategy when you truly can afford it, particularly if you're planning to buy multiple items for which the savings alone would pay for the cost of your travel.

7. **Frequent discount retailers**

Pick up the trendiest looks at stores like Target and H&M. Don't worry that the clothes didn't come from a so-called upscale retailer. Most times, no one will know the difference.

8. **Make mental comparisons**

When you are tempted to plop down a big chunk of money for, say, a cashmere sweater (and yes, I know it's a beautiful one), ask yourself: is this *really* worth a full day's pay? For more expensive items think: is this truly worth a week of my labor? A month's worth?

9. **Do something radical**

If you find yourself at the mall every week (or even every day), plan to make a radical change – if only temporarily. Make a vow to do ABSOLUTELY no shopping whatsoever for an entire month, or for whatever period of time you think you can stand it. You'd be surprised how much strength you can muster up if you put your mind to it. And while you're saving gobs of money in the process, you'll find other creative uses of your time – and cash.

10. **Give something away**

Emulate your favorite celebrity and make a donation to a worthwhile cause. Surely, you have something in the back of your closet or packed away in the attic or basement that you've not worn in a month's worth of Sundays. Give it to a charity like Dress for Success or a woman's shelter. There's truth in the saying: What goes around, comes around. You give something to someone else in need, and your generosity will come back to you in some way. In other words: to get a blessing, first *be* a blessing!

Day 20: Adjust your W-4 withholdings if you get a refund

The IRS says that the average tax refund is around $3,000. If you always get money back from Uncle Sam, it means you're giving the government an interest-free loan.

Refund Checks Show Poor Financial Planning

I don't care how much you enjoy getting that "bonus" once a year. Generally speaking, any time you get a federal tax refund, that demonstrates that there was a lack of proper financial planning on your part. Getting a big refund – no matter how good it feels at the time – isn't smart, and it doesn't make sense. Instead of letting the feds take out extra taxes, keep your money and use it wisely.

A Quick Fix via Your Human Resources Department

Go to your HR department at work and adjust your W-4 withholdings, so that your employer takes out fewer taxes from your paycheck. Your next paycheck will be bigger. Use the extra money to pay down your debt. When you raise your number of withholdings, make sure that you track your level of taxes paid. Don't take out too few taxes and wind up with a big tax bill on April 15th. But if you owe a small amount to the government, that's better than getting a refund; it means you had more cash the previous year.

Interestingly, studies often show that paying off bills is a top priority for people receiving tax refunds. In fact, many people polled specifically say they plan to use their tax refund checks to reduce debt.

Relatively few people plan to splurge and spend the money on things like vacations, clothes or electronics. Of course, there's a lot of evidence that people often say they'll do one thing with their money – and then they wind up *doing* something entirely different. You've probably fallen into this trap at least once, if not regularly. Have you ever planned to do something responsible with your money and then totally blown those bucks? Oftentimes, even the best of intentions can't save us from ourselves if we let our impulses drive our financial decision-making.

Don't let this step turn into one of those ever-growing things on your "I'll do it later" list. Get into that HR office today – or the first day you return to work – and adjust your withholdings.

If you feel unsure about changing your withholdings or if you have questions about the process, pick up a copy of IRS Publication 919. This document will take you through the entire process and explain the correct way to fill out a W-4. Don't worry. It's not terribly complex. It simply boils down to this: When you adjust your W-4 at work, you'll increase the number of allowances that you claim on line five of your W-4 form. Your goal is to decrease the withholding amount so that you ultimately receive a bigger paycheck. Bottom line: if you're constantly receiving annual refund checks, adjusting your W-4 at work will instantly put money in your pocket.

That extra money will immediately get funneled into your paycheck. So let's say you usually get a $2,400 refund, which is close to the average of what many people receive. Well, $2,400 dollars translates into $200 a month that you could be getting right now in your paycheck. If you get paid once every two weeks, expect to see an extra hundred bucks in each paycheck.

Day 21: Sell or donate stuff you don't want, use or need

Want to raise some extra cash in a hurry? Hold a yard sale and unload unwanted electronics, clothing, furniture or other household goods. Get rid of anything you don't want, need or use regularly. These items can also be auctioned on Craigslist or eBay (www.ebay.com). When you get the money from your sales, send it to your creditors to pay down your debt. You can also donate most goods to charity, get a receipt for your contribution, and reap a tax break for your generosity.

Holiday Giving All Year Round

November and December tend to be the months when many people turn their thoughts to charitable giving. However, you don't have to wait until year's end to be generous. But scores of citizens don't get the tax breaks they deserve from their philanthropic efforts simply because they vastly underestimate the value of their donations – or they're among the 66% of Americans who don't itemize their deductions, and therefore can't claim charitable contributions on their federal tax returns.

But with just a little bit of work, you can reap big financial benefits from your generosity.

For many givers, the key is to correctly calculate the total value of your charitable largesse – whether it's cash, or figuring out the worth of a couch, computer monitor, or a man's suit donated to charity.

Here are five suggestions to get the most out of your charitable giving. You may not have big chunks of cash to donate to organizations like the Salvation Army or Red Cross. But if you donate any non-cash items – like clothes, toys, or household goods – you need to figure out the cash value of those items. The IRS isn't known for having simple rules and codes.

But this is one area where Uncle Sam is very clear: you can deduct the going price for an item based on its condition at the time you donate it.

- One way to value your donations is to find out what a local thrift shop or consignment store charges for similar items.

- You can also look at the classified ads in your local newspaper for the price of a similar product. Again, you'll need to take into consideration the condition of your donation. If you're giving a fairly new coat that's in excellent condition, you could adjust the value upward from what others are charging.

- Finally, if you'd rather not call up thrift stores or go through classified listings, you can use a software program, such as ItsDeductible, which has already surveyed average prices nationwide. The ItsDeductible software, owned by Intuit (www.intuit.com), determines and assigns accurate valuations to thousands of commonly donated items. This way, there's no guesswork in valuing your donations – and you can have confidence that you're not overstating the value of your donations. Neither would you be shortchanging yourself by taking deductions that are too modest, as most people do.

The folks at Intuit are so confident that you'll get big returns by using their software that they guarantee that ItsDeductible will save you at least $300 in taxes.

You'd probably be surprised to know what you can legitimately claim for items in good condition that you donate to charity. At last check, a 21' LCD computer monitor was valued at $10, a man's designer three-piece suit $49, a girl's casual dress $8, and a pullover sweater $14, according to ItsDeductible.

- For additional information, get a copy of IRS Publication 561, Determining the Value of Donated Property. You can also call the IRS at 1-800-TAX-FORM and request a free copy of this publication.
- You should always have records to back up your estimates.

For any contribution under $250, keep a receipt from the charity, or your own written record of the donation. It should show the charity's name and address, the date and location of the donation, a description of what you donated, its market value, and the original cost.

If you give something valued above $250, you should have a letter or written acknowledgement from the charity documenting the specifics of your donation, and spelling out any good or services you may have received in exchange for your contribution. For items valued between $501 and $5,000, you should also be prepared, if necessary, to show the IRS records indicating how you originally obtained the property (whether it was a gift, purchase, or inheritance), its original cost, and the approximate date that you obtained the property.

Week 4 Overview

This week, you will:

√ Find a way to generate additional income

√ Apply for a home equity loan or line of credit

√ Refinance your auto loan

√ Pick a "Pay Down Your Debt" priority strategy

√ Consider the pros and cons of debt management programs

√ Evaluate your existing insurance coverage

√ Draw up a will

Day 22: Find a way to generate additional income

Anything you can do to generate other income can go a long way towards reducing your debt – especially if you'd like to wipe out your bills fast. One option is to get a second job, even if only temporarily.

Is a Second Job or Part-Time Work in Your Future?

I realize that most people already work really hard, and often put in more than 40 hours a week on the job. But if you can even fathom the idea, consider getting a second job or part-time work – just for a set period of time, perhaps three months. This may seem like a big sacrifice and a burden. But trust me: it's nothing compared to the burden of carrying around debt year after year. Take every dollar earned from your second job and use it to reduce debt or build an emergency savings fund.

Your emergency fund, or emergency cash cushion, should be at least three times your monthly expenses. In other words, if your bills are $3,000 a month, you should have a $9,000 emergency fund. I know this is hard to amass, but you can build it over time. And, trust me, having a cash cushion is crucial in case one of the five Dreaded Ds (downsizing, divorce, death in the family of the main breadwinner, disability or disease) ever strikes.

Turn a Hobby into Cash

Maybe right now you're saying: *"Lynnette, you have absolutely lost your mind if you think I'm going to go slaving away on a job for even more hours than I do now!"*

Well, if the idea of more work is so unbearable, how about playing for money? And I don't mean hitting the slots or the crap tables in Vegas or Atlantic City. I mean do you have any hobbies – or things you do for fun or entertainment – that you can actually turn into cold, hard cash?

Do you like to knit or sew things? There's a market for that – just go after people who might want hand-made (read: customized or tailored) clothing. Charge your customers enough to cover all your expenses, for fabric, supplies, etc. Then add in a hefty labor charge to make sure the profit you receive is worth your while.

Perhaps you're good at styling or cutting people's hair and you actually like to be creative in that way, as well. Okay, so put the word out in your neighborhood, or among your family and friends, that you'll do hair – for a fee – from the comfort of your home.

Whatever pastime you take pleasure in, chances are there's someone out there willing to pay you for it – regardless of whether you're providing goods or service.

The Small-Office Home-Office Solution

Speaking of goods and services, now may be the time to consider doing something that so many Americans are on the fence to do: *start their own business*. And if millions of entrepreneurs across the country are correct, one of the best ways to launch a business is right out of your own home (or apartment … or garage).

The Ideal Part-Time Enterprise

A word to you dreamers out there: don't look at this advice and go off half-cocked, talking to your spouse about how you're going to start raising ostriches and make $100,000 a year at it – and I don't care if you happen to live on a farm! In all cases, you want to home-in on no-cost or low-cost ventures businesses that you can do by yourself, and if possible, start-ups that can be operated exclusively or mainly from the privacy of your own home.

Why these characteristics? For starters, you don't have the money to buy tons of products. You also don't want to have to hire anybody. Hey, you need to keep all the money you'll earn, don't you? And by taking the home-based approach, you won't have to pay extra money to lease space or rent a place from which you'll run your home-based business (you're already paying something to live where you are, right?). Running the business from home also means no commuting costs or commuting time (unless you call the 30-second walk from your bedroom to your basement a serious commute).

Leverage the Internet

Finally, if you're a person who is web-savvy, I'd encourage you by all means to harness the power of the Internet to make money in any way possible – any way that's legal and moral, of course. For instance, maybe you're a good writer. Scores of corporations and organizations out there need writers to – well, write – all kinds of stuff: pamphlets, brochures, company newsletters, employment manuals, etc. Some examples include Upwork, Fiverr, Freelancer.com, and so forth.

You can offer to do desktop publishing services if you have a penchant for that. Perhaps you speak another language: think about selling online language instruction. With the Internet as your gateway, your customer base is almost unlimited. Clients can be in any parts of the world – as long as they're willing to hire you, and pay up in a timely manner.

Squeezing Money out of Where You Live

Another way to generate income is to consider getting a roommate and/or renting a room in your apartment, house, attic or basement.

If you're a renter, be sure not to violate your rental contract. But if nothing in your renter's agreement prohibits you for letting someone else live with you, you might think about whether having an extra body around the house can help you out of a financial jam. Obviously if you own your own home, you don't have to ask anyone's permission to take on a tenant. Well, you should get the okay from your spouse before you go taking out "For Rent" ads in the local paper. Aside from that, though, the big question is probably this: could you tolerate having an extra person around your house all the time? If your answer is yes, then you may have found a viable strategy to lighten the cost of your mortgage and utilities. Lots of people want to just rent a room – especially in expensive areas of the country, like on the East and West Coasts. But even in other regions of the U.S., tenants who need a safe, affordable place over their heads may be plentiful. And by renting out a room, from you, they'll save money by not having to pay the entire cost of renting their own apartment or paying their own mortgage. Websites like Airbnb and VRBO.com can offer your home for temporary tenants, staying as short as a day or as long as you wish.

If the idea of a permanent or full-time tenant appeals to you about as much as the thought of spending all day in line at the Department of Motor Vehicles, maybe you could just rent out your place temporarily. For example, you might rent your place to others during the holidays, a busy travel season, or during the summer, if you're away from home.

If you follow these guidelines, and are willing to think creatively about how you can pad your current income – without killing yourself in the process – you can slash your debts by leaps and bounds and become financially fit much, much faster.

Day 23: Apply for a home equity loan or equity line of credit.

If you have equity in your house, it can be a wise strategy to use a home equity loan to pay off your credit card debt. The interest you pay on mortgage debt is tax-deductible, up to $100,000, and mortgages typically carry much lower interest rates than credit card debt. But, caution: don't pay off those credit card bills, and put your home at risk with an equity loan if you're just going to go back out and run up your charge cards again.

The decision to take out a home equity loan is one that should not be made lightly. I believe that you should only use your home equity to pay off debt under two circumstances:

1) You got into credit card debt because of the Dreaded D's (downsizing, divorce, disability, etc.) or some other personal disaster, like a business failure or lawsuit; and

2) The situation that threw you into debt has now been rectified. (For instance, you were downsized, but now you have a job, or you faced a disease or a disability, but now you've bounced back from your medical problems).

If you got into debt for other reasons of your own doing, such as over- spending, and if you haven't learned how to get those impulses under control, I urge you to refrain from tapping the equity in your home to pay off credit card debt. I've heard heart-breaking stories of people who paid off their credit card debts by converting those obligations into mortgage debt – only to keep spending, not change their financial habits, and ultimately wind up losing their homes in foreclosure. I don't want this to happen to you.

The Financial Benefits of Owning Real Estate

Home ownership is critical to your financial security. In my third book, *The Money Coach's Guide to Your First Million*, I pointed out that for more than 90% of all millionaires in the U.S., real estate is a cornerstone of their wealth. Owning real estate – either your principal residence and/ or investment property – has terrific financial advantages. You get tax breaks for paying property taxes and mortgage interest. You get regular income and can take a depreciation deduction for rental property. If you have a home-based business, the tax breaks are even juicier; Uncle Sam lets you write off a variety of expenses associated with running your business from the comfort of your abode.

As a homeowner, you also get the chance to enjoy price appreciation, something that's happened — more often than not — with residential real estate throughout the country over several decades. For instance, in the first 39 years that the National Association of Realtors has tracked single- family home prices, they went up every single year. Even in 2006, when the real estate market cooled off considerably, the price of the average single family home still rose by 1.1%, to $222,100. Despite the recession of 2008 (and the subsequent real-estate bubble), average home prices have steadily returned to pre-recession levels. The national median existing single-family home price in the second quarter of 2016 was $240,700, NAR data show.

In addition, low mortgages rates – well below 4% in 2016 – have made buying a home a solid investment.

For these reasons and more, you've probably heard it said that renting an apartment is simply "throwing your money away" month after month. I believe that it's actually worse than that. It's not just that you're losing out on a multitude of financial incentives.

Renting a home or an apartment puts you at a big disadvantage in other ways. Home ownership often affords you rights and freedoms that renters don't have. For instance, you can paint the inside of your house any color you want, hang paintings on the wall wherever you'd like, or have a cat or dog if you so choose. If you're renting, though, you have to get a landlord's permission to do these things– not always an easy task. Home ownership also has considerable intangible benefits – like the pride you get from being a homeowner (don't you love it when visitors compliment you on your beautiful garden?) or the sense of satisfaction you feel just knowing you're setting a good example for young people and others who aspire to home ownership. Lastly, a home provides more than just a roof over your head each night or a meeting place for family gatherings. It can become part of your legacy – an asset that you own free and clear and perhaps leave to your children or grandchildren.

Unfortunately, too many people are using up the equity in their homes at unprecedented levels. That worries me greatly. Fifty years ago, Americans averaged about 85% equity in their homes, net of debt. Before the real estate bubble burst and the recession that followed, that figure was around 38% in 2006, according to George Marotta, a NAPFA- registered financial advisor and research fellow at Stanford University's Hoover Institution. In 2016, that number was closer to 70%.

The problem is that people who lack proper money management skills are getting cash-out mortgage refinancing to pay off debts and make various expenditures. My concern is that at some point, many individuals will find themselves in situations where the homes that were keeping them afloat start to sink under a boatload of debts. This is especially true for those in the later years of life, many of whom have a disproportionate amount of net worth in their homes, not in their other assets and balances.

What's the Difference between a Home Equity Loan and a Home Equity Line of Credit?

Having duly warned you about the perils of tapping your home's equity, let me now reiterate that using mortgage debt to pay off consumer debt –like credit cards and auto loans – can be a smart thing to do. Just make sure your spending patterns and money habits won't get you into financial trouble again. And if you heed the advice contained in *Zero Debt*, you shouldn't have a problem.

To tap the equity in your home, you'll have to decide whether you need a home equity loan or an equity line of credit. An equity loan is best if you require one big lump sum – like paying off all your debts in one fell swoop. You'll then have to start paying back the entire amount borrowed. With an equity line of credit, you have access to funds, up to your maximum credit available, but you don't pay back any money until you actually use the funds. Also, with an equity line of credit you use checks to draw upon your available credit. When you have those checks, it can be tempting to use them for any number of reasons. But don't make the mistake that so many people do, of using your home equity line of credit to pay for your normal monthly bills or your daily living expenses. That's an imprudent use of your home equity, and hazardous to your personal wealth.

Need A Mortgage? Credit Re-Scoring Can Help

If you're applying for a new mortgage or are refinancing and think you may get turned down because of inaccurate, outdated or negative information on your credit report, make sure you go with a lender who knows about "credit re-scoring."

Here's how it works. If you have a mortgage application pending, and you know there are mistakes in your credit file, your lender (via a third- party rapid re-scoring firm, like Avantus) submits proof of the error to the credit bureaus. Equifax, Experian and TransUnion all have special departments set up to deal with these requests on an expedited basis.

After receiving the proper proof of the mistake, the credit bureau updates your credit file. No one guarantees that your FICO score will be raised, but experts in the field say that most times, it works. Among the types of information that can be corrected are:

- Collection accounts still showing an unpaid status
- Judgments or tax liens that have been paid or satisfied
- Payments erroneously reported as late, or changes in account status, such as from "delinquent" to "current"
- Debts that should be included in a discharged bankruptcy
- Accounts that were paid and closed but still show a balance

Only mortgage lenders can initiate the rapid re-scoring process with the credit bureaus. Individuals can't do it. According to Credit Communications Inc., a credit re-scoring firm, the credit bureaus only accept official documents as proof of mistakes, such as:

- A letter from the creditor or collection agency. (And it must have the same account number on the letter or receipt as is being reported by the credit bureaus)
- Certified satisfaction of judgment from a court
- Certified tax lien release from the IRS

- Certified bankruptcy discharge papers from a court
- The bureaus will not accept the following documentation: canceled checks, receipts for money orders, account statements, hand- written letters, third party documentation, and other unverifiable documents

The rapid re-scoring process can be a powerful way to quickly improve your credit profile in as little as 48 hours. Again, it's only for those in the market for a mortgage, and the updates are only made when there are errors in your credit report.

What Are Reverse Mortgages?

For those of you who are aged 62 and over, another method of freeing up some cash to pay off your credit card debts (and yes, older people have increasing amounts of debt too!) is to consider a reverse mortgage. Here's what a reverse mortgage is and how it can be used to your benefit.

A traditional mortgage represents an obligation on your part, where you pay a monthly payment to a bank or mortgage company over a fixed number of years. The more money you pay, the more equity you build up in the house. After a set time, say 30 years, you own the home outright when all of the payments have been made. A reverse mortgage is still a loan against your house, but it works the opposite way: instead of you paying the bank, the bank pays you a fixed stream of money until you or the last surviving borrower dies or sells the home. The loan the bank provides can be in the form of upfront money and/or regular monthly payments. This loan doesn't have to be repaid for as long as you live in the house. Over time, the more money the bank pays/lends you, the larger your debt becomes. With each payment you collect from the bank, your equity in the house is reduced. A reverse mortgage lender will analyze your situation and tell you how big a loan you'd qualify for, based on your age and your home's value.

To get a reverse mortgage, you must meet these criteria:

- You must be at least 62 years old and living in your home as your primary place of residence.
- Your home must be a single-family residence in a 1-to-4 unit building, condominium or part of a planned unit development. Manufactured homes qualify, but most co-ops and mobile homes don't.
- Your home must be at least one year old and meet HUD's property standards. However, if you need the money to pay for required repairs, you can still qualify.
- You must not have any debt against your property. To meet this rule, most people simply get a cash advance from the reverse mortgage and use the money to pay off any existing loans/mortgages against their property.
- You must go through reverse-mortgage counseling to make sure you understand this loan product.

The Pros and Cons of Reverse Mortgages

As America's retirees and aging baby boomer population grapple with rising medical costs, retirement portfolios battered by the stock market, and increased personal debt, more and more people are turning to reverse mortgages as a way to have adequate cash flow. But senior citizens and others have lots of misconceptions about reverse mortgages. Perhaps the biggest myth is that you could lose your home. The truth is that you can't. Nor can you wind up owing more than the home is worth; federal law prohibits this. After you die or sell your home, if you had a reverse mortgage, the amount to be paid back to the bank is the total of the payments you received plus interest. Another misconception about these loans is that the borrower gives up ownership of the home. In reality, if you get a reverse mortgage, you keep title and ownership of your house. The bank, however, does get a lien against the property. If you or someone you know is thinking about getting a reverse mortgage, be sure you weigh the following pros and cons. Here are the positive factors concerning reverse mortgages:

- The money can be used for any purpose you want.
- These loans are available in all 50 states, including the District of Columbia and Puerto Rico.
- Income, employment and credit standing are not considerations, since you don't have to repay anything.

Now here are the negative factors concerning reverse mortgages:

- You won't be able to leave the home free and clear for your kids. In most cases, the loan is paid back after the borrower's death by selling the property.
- The cost of getting a reverse mortgage can be quite high. Origination fees can run as much as 2%. Also, mortgage insurance – which is mandatory for these loans – may total another 2%. Expect other fees: title insurance, appraisal etc.

For more information on this topic, check out a publication from the AARP called "Home Made Money: A Consumer's Guide to Reverse

Mortgages." You can find it at the organization's website, www. aarp.org, or by calling the AARP membership line at 888-687-2277. The industry's trade group, the National Reverse Mortgage Lenders Association, also has three helpful consumer guides: "Just the FAQs: Answers to Common Questions About Reverse Mortgages;" "Using Reverse Mortgages for Healthcare: An NRMLA Guide;" and "The NRMLA Consumer Guide to Reverse Mortgages." All are free and can be downloaded from the group's website at www.nrmlaonline. org. You can also contact the NRMLA by telephone at 866-264-4466 to order these informative publications.

Day 24: Refinance your auto loan

When you're trying to achieve Zero Debt status and financial freedom, remember to consider all types of debt: your mortgages, auto loans, credit cards, student loans, etc. Anytime you buy a car, realize that you're purchasing a depreciating asset. <u>Translation</u>: as soon as you drive that new or used vehicle off the dealer's lot, it immediately starts to lose value. Nobody ever re-sells a car for more than they paid for it. That makes a car different from assets like a home or stocks, where you expect to later sell them for more than your purchase price. So if you're making car payments, it's really important to manage this debt wisely. If you can't pay 100% cash for your new wheels (and most people don't), then at least be a savvy consumer when obtaining an auto loan. Your goal is to save money, and to avoid any negative marks on your credit that can result from missing car payments or having your car repossessed. Fortunately, vehicle financing is one area where you can cut your expenses (and keep the Repo Man at bay) with a little know-how and some simple action.

Many people don't know that you can refinance your car loan, just as you can refinance a mortgage. But a car refinancing is easier, faster and requires no points, appraisal or closing costs. For this reason, auto refinancing has been called "one of the best-kept secrets in personal finance."

To lower your car payments, turn to Capital One Auto Finance (www.capitalone.com), the top online vehicle lender in the United States. Refinancing takes just 15 minutes and saves an average of about $700 over the life of the loan. What will you do with the money you save? Pay down all your other debts, naturally.

The Capital One Advantage

If you're in the market to buy a new or used car or motorcycle, Capital One Auto also offers you a blank check to buy the vehicle and give you more negotiating power at a car dealership.

Take the case of Jim Adsley. Adsley thought he got a good deal when he bought a used Cadillac with 8.25% financing through GMAC. But later, he found an even better bargain, by refinancing his auto loan at a 6.9% rate.

"I'll save about $3,500" over the life of the loan, says Adsley, a retiree from Langley, WA, who used Capital One Auto.

All across the country, scores of consumers like Adsley are refinancing their car loans – prompted by the same low interest rate environment that encourages homeowners to refinance their mortgages. But one benefit of refinancing your auto loans is that, unlike refinancing a home loan, there are no points to pay and no appraisal required. So you can save a lot of money.

You generate savings in one of two ways. You can simply refinance your current loan if interest rates are lower than they were when you bought your car. Or you can extend the life of your auto loan, spreading your payments over a longer time period and thereby lowering your monthly car bill. Some people do both. Every year, hundreds of thousands of people refinance their auto loans, and altogether there are tens of billions of these loans outstanding, according to CNW Marketing Research.

Online Lenders Dominate Auto Refinancing

Currently, hundreds of lenders nationwide offer auto refinancing. Many are online companies, such as Eloan.com and LendingTree.com.

One of the biggest players in the business, though, is Capital One Auto a unit of Capital One Financial.

At CapitalOne.com, you fill out an online application, providing information about your current monthly car payment, interest rate, and balance due. The company immediately performs a credit check, and if you apply during normal business hours, you receive an e-mail answer within 15 minutes. If you're approved, the message will state your new monthly payment and revised interest rate. (Note: It pays to have good credit: as of September 2016, CapitalOneAuto's best auto refinancing rate was 2.99% for auto refinance loans. After approval, the company mails you a check to pay off your existing car loan). Then you start making new payments to CapitalOneAuto.com. For any auto refinancing, you'll pay a lien transfer fee. It's between $5 and $65, depending on the state in which you live.

Capital One does not offer financing for motorcycles, vehicles older than seven years, cars with more than 70,000 miles (120,000 if through dealer), or automobiles purchased from individuals in a private party or person-to-person sale.

Beware Of Extending Your Loan Length

While auto refinancing offers savings and speed, it also has potential downsides, if you extend the life of your car loan unnecessarily. For instance, say you bought a car three years ago and originally had a five-year loan. You now have only two years left before you own the vehicle free and clear. But if you refinanced by taking out a new five-year loan, you'd be tacking on another three years of payments – extra interest and all. Additionally, any warranty covering your car could expire before you finish paying off your new loan.

That's why auto refinancing typically makes the most sense for new loans where you feel a dealer or finance company dinged you on the interest rate charged. Refinancing can also be advantageous if you've been paying on your current auto loan for a year or two, and you don't plan to extend your repayment term.

Finally, refinancing is worth pursuing if you had past credit problems that have since been resolved. Your improved credit standing makes you a better bank risk, and should get you a reduced interest rate.

Day 25: Pick a Proper Debt Payoff Strategy

Trying to dig out of credit card debt can often feel like treading water. Although you're making those payments every month, you still can't seem to get ahead. Unfortunately, lots of you grappling with credit card bills thwart your efforts to become debt-free by making a huge financial mistake: even though you barely see your balances budge, you continue to pay off their credit cards with the highest interest rate first, under the assumption that doing so is always the best way to have zero debt. In reality, nothing could be farther from the truth.

I know this is going to sound like financial heresy to many of you. After all, every personal finance book you've read and every financial expert you've heard discuss this subject has said the same thing: pay off high interest rate debt first. Well, I hate to shock you, but there's a huge problem with this age-old advice: it doesn't work for most people. Even worse, following this well-intentioned but misguided advice could cost you money, damage your credit rating, and put your financial health at risk in unintended ways.

Let me first explain why the oft-heard admonition to focus on your high-interest-rate debt is misinformed. Then I'll tell you a better way to prioritize your debts and choose the most effective method way to pay off your credit card bills. Trust me: when you're done reading this section, you may have an "Aha" moment about why you haven't been able to pay down your credit cards bills faster.

Four Enormous (and Wrong) Assumptions

When personal finance gurus advise you to pay off high interest rate debt first, they are making the assumption that:

- the interest rates on your credit card are high
- you are bothered by your credit card interest rates
- this strategy is the fastest route to paying off your debts
- you'll save the most amount of money by using this technique

These are four enormous assumptions. Unfortunately, for millions of Americans who are deep in debt, these suppositions are flat-out wrong. Here's why.

Be Glad the 1980s Are Gone

For starters, credit card interest rates are not at sky high levels. Most lenders use the prime rate as their benchmark for setting interest rates on credit cards, home equity lines, auto loans and other personal consumer loans. The prime rate is based on the federal funds rate. Set by the Federal Reserve, the fed funds rate is the rate that banks charge one another to borrow money overnight. As of today, the prime rate in the United States stands at 3.5%, with the fed funds rate at 0.5%. As a result, standard credit cards with fixed interest rates average 13%, while credit cards with variable interest rates average 15%, according to CreditCards.com. By comparison, the prime rate peaked at 21.5% in December 1980, and in the mid-1980s, credit card interest rates averaged a record 18.75%.

What's Really Bugging You?

When it comes to your credit cards, think for a moment about what really drives you nuts. Most financial advisers make the erroneous assumption that all consumers are upset about high interest rates, but often that is not the case at all. I remember when I had $100,000 in credit card debt back in 2001. Fortunately, I managed to pay off my debts in three years without ever missing a payment. Because of my track record, I had leverage to negotiate with my credit card companies. I asked for, and received, lower interest rates on nearly all my credit cards. At one point, none of my cards carried an interest rate above 6.9%. In fact, several cards had 0% interest, while others were at 2.9% or 4.9%. In short, I wasn't bothered at all by my interest rates, because they were very manageable.

High Dollar Balances

What did bother me, however, was that my cards all had high dollar balances. Because I'd been an over-spender, I was maxed out on many credit cards, and those cards that weren't maxed out were approaching their limits. Imagine my angst when I had the nerve to go out to dinner at some fancy New York restaurant. Despite the risk of public embarrassment, I'd plunk down a credit card to pay for the bill and then had to cross my fingers – and say a silent prayer – in the hopes that the card would be approved!

True Story: $1 Million in Credit Card Debt

When I worked as a *Wall Street Journal* reporter for CNBC in the early 2000s, I interviewed a gentleman who was then the president of the National Foundation for Credit Counseling. The NFCC is the parent company of Consumer Credit Counseling Service, the nation's oldest and largest non-profit credit counseling agency.

I don't remember the president's name, but I'll never forget the story he told me a story about a client – a Wall Street professional – who came to the NFCC with a whopping $1 million worth of credit card debt. Intrigued by this case, I asked whether the NFCC helped this man by negotiating lower interest rates on his cards. The former NFCC president told me "No," because the man wasn't concerned about his interest rates. I then asked whether the client was stressed out by the huge dollar amount that he owed. Again, the answer was "No." "Even though he had a million dollars in debt, he also earned a million dollars a year," I was told. Confused, I asked: "Well what was his problem?"

Too Many Credit Cards

I then learned that this deeply indebted man was most troubled by the sheer number of credit card accounts he had. It turns out the guy owned more than three-dozen credit cards, and he found it overwhelming just to keep up with all the monthly statements, the paperwork, making the payments on time – not to mention that his wife didn't know about all the cards. Like me, this man was heavily in debt. But the solution to his problem wasn't tied to him paying off high-rate debt first. To suggest that option to this man would've been like trying to give an aspirin to a patient with a brain tumor. While an aspirin will help cure many headaches, it won't alleviate a brain tumor victim's woes, because an aspirin isn't attacking the true source of the pain. Likewise, a recommendation to "always pay your high rate debt first" often doesn't work because it represents a one- size-fits-all financial strategy force-fed to consumers without regard for what really ails them.

The Myth of the Speedier Repayments

What about the assumption that paying off high interest rate credit card debt first will get rid of your credit card bills fastest? Again, this is a fallacy that's not supported by reality. Clearly, paying off one's debts isn't as simple as tackling your high interest rate credit cards first. If that worked, we would see far more people using this strategy successfully eliminating their debts, as opposed to languishing in debt year after year. We also probably wouldn't have had millions of American households file for bankruptcy protection in recent years (mainly due to credit card debt), and credit card delinquencies on the rise yet again.

Even credit counseling agencies, which also encourage consumers to first deal with higher rate debt, acknowledge that individuals in credit counseling programs who take this advice often fail to successfully repay their bills, let alone do it quickly. The average credit counseling/debt management plan lasts about four years. Yet, most consumers fail to complete such programs. According to information provided by the credit counseling agencies (NFCC and Cambridge Credit Counseling), the average completion rate hovers around 20%. While I think the NFCC is a worthwhile program, I also think one-in-five odds stink. Part of the problem may be that consumers are being urged to pay off their debts in a way that doesn't make sense for them. The "pay your high rate debt first" strategy isn't addressing their pain, so consumers are getting discouraged and they ultimately give up.

What About the Cost Savings?

Some readers will no doubt take issue with me, insisting that paying off high-rate debt first will surely result in the greatest cost savings, if only consumers would follow through with the advice. My answer: that's a monumental IF. And therein lies the problem.

If people consistently paid off high-rate debt first, would that save them the most amount of money in the long-run? Yes, it likely would. But the truth of the matter is that most people don't consistently pay off their high-rate debt, because, as explained, most people may not be suffering from crushing interest rates. So telling someone to just worry about the high-rate debt first is almost setting them up for failure. If you've ever wondered why this hasn't worked for you, or why you haven't been able to stick to a debt payoff plan, it could be that you aren't sufficiently motivated to merely "pay off high interest rate credit cards first."

Ill-Guided Advice Leads to Frustrated Consumers

For example, take the case of a woman who's really worried about the high dollar balances on her credit cards. She may have three cards, one with a 6.9% teaser rate and a $7,000 balance, another with at interest rates of 13.9% and a $5,500 balance, and a third card at 18.9% with a $3,000 balance.

Conventional wisdom would dictate that she aggressively pay off the 18.9% card first. Meanwhile, this woman is actually fretting over her lower- rate cards that are approaching their limits. Nevertheless, she allocates $400 monthly to credit card repayments, putting $100 apiece on the first two cards, and $200 on the highest-rate card. Every time she does this, however, she stresses out over her lower-rate cards with the bigger balances. The $100 a month just covers the minimum payment on those cards, and every time she gets her statement, those balances barely seem to have budged at all.

Frustrated, she closes the accounts and vows not to use credit cards any more – a move that actually hurts her FICO credit score. The end result for this woman, like millions of consumers, is the same: When people aren't motivated to stick to a payoff strategy, they won't do it month in and month out until they knock out their debts. In the end, they pay bills late, or not at all, risking further damage to their credit files and jeopardizing their financial health. This is no different from a woman who enrolls in a fitness gym to lose weight, and gets constantly put on the treadmill, or shoe-horned into other activities she doesn't like. Without the right motivation, she won't stick to the plan; nor will she lose weight.

Pick a Proper Debt Payoff Strategy

Here's a better way to become debt-free: Choose a payoff strategy that attacks your area of pain. This will give you both the emotional satisfaction and the economic reward of paying off your debts. As a result, you'll stay motivated enough to stick to your repayment plan. In the end, this is what will help you to have zero balances on your credit card statements.

There are three primary payoff techniques you can select, based on what ails you most.

1. **Deal with Killer Interest Rates**

   If you're facing exorbitant interest rates and they're killing you, then yes, by all means, concentrate on the high-rate debt first. This may be the case if you have a wallet full of store-brand cards, from retailers. These cards typically carry much higher interest rates than national brand cards, such as Visa, MasterCard or Discover. Also, if you've had credit problems in the past, or if you've been recently late on your card payments, you may be stuck with "default" interest rates, which can easily top 22% and can sometimes run as high as 30%. If any of these scenarios describe you, and if you're losing sleep at night because of your high interest rates, then you should pay down those debts first.

2. Attack Cards with High Dollar Balances

For those of you on edge about being so close to your credit limits, the best repayment strategy is to first focus on those cards with high dollar balances. In the case of the woman described above, instead of worrying about the card with the 18.9% interest rate, she should attack the card with the highest dollar balance, the one with $7,500 due. By paying extra on that card first, she'll get the psychic satisfaction of watching that balance drop measurably each month – which is the emotional relief she needs to keep paying off the debt.

3. Get Relief from Multiple Accounts

Perhaps you're actually like the Wall Street pro I mentioned earlier. Not the million dollars in debt part – the part about struggling to juggle multiple accounts. Some ways to know if you have way too many credit card accounts are if you find it hard to keep up with your paperwork, if you forget about bills, or if you often get dinged with late fees just because you didn't write or mail out all your checks on time. Does any of this sound familiar? If so, the best solution for you is to first go after the cards with the lowest dollar balances. This way you'll quickly knock out cards with small balances. Each time you do eliminate a card, you'll use the money you were paying on that card to double up on the next card with the smallest balance. In this fashion, you'll get a two-fold benefit: You reap the pleasure of watching the number of accounts you have rapidly decline, and your overall debt balances will dwindle, as well.

The overall lesson here is to do what works for your individual situation – taking into account not just your financial needs, but your emotional ones, too. Pick a debt repayment strategy that will rid you of your worries about credit card debt and give you the satisfaction of seeing – month after month – that your bills aren't insurmountable. That's the repayment plan you'll stick with, and that's also the method that will help you to most quickly become debt-free.

So here's your plan: Decide whether you are most upset by having big balances, high interest rates, or multiple accounts.

Solution: review the list of creditors you created on **Day 3**.

Strategy 1: If you despise high interest rates, start by paying off the card with *the largest rate*, no matter the balance.

Strategy 2: If you want to knock out large debts, attack the card with the *biggest dollar balance* first, regardless of the interest rate.

Strategy 3: If you're tired of juggling too many cards, first pay off the card with the *lowest dollar balance*.

As you attack your area of pain, you'll first pay off the card that's bothering you most. Then repeat this process to eliminate the debt on each additional credit card.

Let's see how this strategy works in practice. Say you have five credit cards with the following rates and balances:

- American Express – 15.9% interest rate; $2,300 due
- Visa – 9.9% interest rate: $4,800 due
- MasterCard – 13.9% interest rate; $1,400 due
- Macy's – 21.9% interest rate; $750 due
- Discover – 6.9% interest rate; $6,600 due

Scenario 1: Let's say it drives you nuts to see that you're being charged tons of interest on your purchases. This time, your goal is to pay off *the highest-interest rate* debt first (Strategy 1). So your prioritized repayment schedule looks like this: Pay off Macy's first. It's got that hefty 21.9% interest rate. Then pay American Express. It's carrying a 15.9% interest rate. MasterCard would be your next target; it's got a 13.9% interest rate. The Visa bill follows, with a 9.9% interest rate. And the last credit card you'd pay would be Discover, which has a relatively small 6.9% interest rate.

Scenario 2: I'm going to assume that you're in the second category of consumers: you absolutely abhor seeing big balances, so you'll get really motivated about knocking out your debt with the largest dollar amount due. In this case, you want to attack *the biggest dollar balances* first (Strategy 2). That means you'd first pay off that Discover Card: It has the biggest balance: $6,600. Note that you're paying off Discover first, even though it actually has the lowest interest rate attached to it. After Discover, you pay off the Visa bill ($4,800), then American Express ($2,300); MasterCard ($1,400); and, finally, Macy's ($750).

Scenario 3: Are you feeling overwhelmed and stressed out simply because you have too many accounts and you're finding it hard to juggle all of them? If this describes you, then your best bet is to start knocking out the number of credit cards with balances. You do this by paying off the cards with *the smallest dollar balance* first (Strategy 3). Put into practice, here's how your repayment plan would go: The Macy's bill gets paid first, because that's the smallest total bill outstanding at just $750. Then you pay off the MasterCard ($1,400 due), your American Express card ($2,300 due), that Visa bill ($4,800), and lastly your Discover card, on which you owe $6,600.

What This Technique Does & Does Not Accomplish

You and millions of other people out there are sick with debt. You can't all possibly employ the same exact approach and do equally well. Everyone is different. And I'm betting that you don't want a band-aid for a problem that's really not bothering you. What you want is for the pain to go away: plain and simple. So you need to attack the area that hurts or bothers you – financially, psychically, whatever – and then keep pressing on to relieve that area of discomfort.

So will my debt payoff strategy mean every consumer will always pay as little as possible in interest? No, it doesn't ensure that at all. It does, however, give every one of you the chance to limit – in your own way – the emotional cost of debt, by empowering you to reclaim your finances, in a method that's most appropriate and comfortable for you.

Day 26: Weigh the pros and cons of debt management plans

If you get nowhere negotiating with your creditors, you're drowning in debt, you've analyzed your budget, cut back on expenses, have implemented the suggestions found in *Zero Debt,* and have still concluded there's no way you can afford to pay all your obligations, the good news is that a debt management program may help. The bad news is that many of them might also hurt you.

Credit Counselors: Friend or Foe?

Every year, about 5 million consumers seek help from debt counseling agencies. The typical person in a debt-management program earns about $35,000 a year, is college-educated and has credit card debts of about $20,000. Obviously these individuals are in a bind.

Unfortunately, the very places they go for help – credit counseling agencies – sometimes make their situations worse. In recent years, complaints about the credit counseling industry have skyrocketed, according to the Better Business Bureau. Over the years, the IRS has audited some 50 credit-counseling agencies to see if they deserve their tax-exempt status. And guess what? Many of them got their tax-exempt status revoked.

The Federal Trade Commission and five state Attorneys General in 2003 sued AmeriDebt and its founder, Andris Pukke, accusing them of misleading 400,000 customers and charging clients $170 million in hidden fees. AmeriDebt went out of business, Pukke went bankrupt, but in 2006 the FTC won a $35 million settlement in the case. However, in 2007, a judge found Pukke in contempt of court for hiding assets, after the FTC alleged that Pukke had made only about $10 million in restitution.

Meanwhile, two other companies, Amerix and Cambridge Credit Counseling, were investigated by a Senate subcommittee. Although they denied wrongdoing, Congress nevertheless recently examined many debt management companies for a variety of alleged wrongful practices including:

- taking clients' money and then not paying their bills
- charging unreasonably high startup/monthly fees
- not disclosing to consumers what fees are going to the debt management company and how much towards bills

Shop around and you'll find that some debt consolidation companies make outrageous claims, even going so far as to promise they'll "fix" your credit report virtually overnight. Any quick-fix company is probably too good to be true. Despite actions undertaken by state and federal laws, the companies still exist to defraud consumers. Consumers, in turn, *frequently* sue these companies for damages to their finances AND their unknowing involvement in quasi-identity-theft schemes. Various scams and regulatory actions were taken against debt help companies in 2016 too.

For these reasons, you need to be especially careful about choosing a credit counseling or debt management company. The credit counseling industry continues to grow by leaps and bounds. Just do a Google search on the phrase "credit counseling" and you'll get roughly 10 million hits. Ditto for the term "debt management," with 6 million hits. And because Congress passed a federal law requiring anyone who files bankruptcy to first receive debt counseling, the industry is poised for even more explosive growth.

In picking a credit counseling agency, at the very least you should make sure that any company you do business with is on the Department of Justice U.S. Trustee Program list of approved credit counselors. These firms have been vetted, somewhat, and are approved to provide you with pre-discharge bankruptcy information and post-bankruptcy credit education. Any legitimate credit counselor will be on the U.S. Trustee list. If an agency isn't listed, don't do business with them. You can find a list of approved credit counselors in your areas by logging onto this website: http://www.usdoj.gov/ust/eo/bapcpa/ccde/cc_approved.htm.

The main problem with the $7 billion debt management industry is that, over the past decade, it has undergone a drastic transformation that is not in consumers' best interests. Let me tell you about the roots of this industry and explain how it now operates. Then I'll tell you the Do's and Don'ts of using a debt management program, in case you decide you need this service.

Traditional Credit Counseling On the Decline

There was a time when people with overwhelming money problems would go to a credit counselor and receive quality advice, help and personal finance education. A person struggling to pay his or her bills might've been signed up for a free class on budgeting, taught the value of saving money for a rainy day, or counseled about how credit cards work. Unfortunately, that has all changed. Lots of programs that used to be free now impose charges. And if you seek help today for your debt woes, 9 times out of 10 you won't get traditional "credit counseling," which was educational in nature. Instead, you're more likely to be funneled into a "debt management program", where your bills are consolidated and you're put on a repayment plan. The problem is that lots of people may not need to enter a debt management plan, also known as a DMP. What many consumers really need is financial education; they need to learn how to manage their budget, credit and spending.

The reason the vast majority of debtors are guided into debt management programs is that these plans are a source of revenue for credit counseling agencies. Despite the fact that most of them are non- profits, they still need money to operate. And they get some of that money from consumers who are on monthly repayment plans.

The Financial Ties That Bind

Unbeknownst to most consumers, credit counseling agencies also get most of their operating expenses from credit card companies, in the form of payments known as "fair share" contributions. Believe it or not, it was the credit card industry that actually set up the whole credit counseling industry a few decades ago. The goal was to make sure people with large debts didn't go bankrupt – thereby writing off all their bills and never paying their creditors a dime. Instead of that happening, credit card companies realized it was better to let people arrange settlements, where they could have reduced payments, pay lower interest rates, and get late fees eliminated.

So creditors funded credit-counseling agencies, thereby helping themselves as they also helped consumers avoid bankruptcy. The payments credit issuers make to debt counseling agencies actually come from you. Whenever you make a payment under your debt management program, your creditor takes a certain percentage of that money and uses it to pay your credit-counseling firm. Credit issuers used to give debt management companies "fair share" payments of about 15% of a consumer's debt. Now most creditors make contributions of just 3% of a person's debt.

To combat unethical practices, The Coalition for Responsible Credit Practices—an organization comprised of credit counseling agencies, business leaders and other—has taken measures to reform the credit counseling industry. Michael Barnhart, the Coalition's executive director, asks: "How can consumers be confident that they are receiving accurate, unbiased advice from agencies that are beholden to creditors for a significant portion of their revenue?" His conclusion: "They obviously cannot."

How Debt Management Programs Work

With most debt management programs here's what you'll have to do: cut up your credit cards; agree to not open any new credit accounts, and make regular payments to the credit counseling agency. They negotiate with your creditors to get your bills slashed and consolidate your debts, allowing you write one monthly check to the agency, which, in turn, sends the money to each of your creditors. Most debt management plans last three or four years.

Do's and Don'ts of Debt Management Plans

I recommend that you first try to negotiate with your creditors on your own. If that fails, and you can't meet your bills despite your best efforts, you may be a good candidate for debt consolidation – as long as you first educate yourself about the process and the debt management or credit counseling company you hire to work on your behalf.

Don't think that just because a company is a non-profit it is "better" than for-profit groups. For starters, most debt counseling agencies are non-profit, but many have ties to for-profit entities. Also, non-profit status tells you nothing about an agency's quality of service. Don't sign any contracts until you get detailed feedback about what your repayment plan will look like and what your fees will be. Don't enroll in any program that costs more than $50 to set up or has monthly fees higher than $25. Don't go with a company that only seems to be pushing debt management plans, or that doesn't seem interested in fully hearing your situation. Some suggest DMPs within the first 15 minutes of your consultation. Better companies talk to you for at least 30 minutes or an hour to get a complete picture of your finances. Also, don't give your bank account information to a debt- counseling firm before you've signed a contract. And finally, don't respond instantly to aggressive marketing pitches – like Spam in your email inbox, Internet advertising or late-night television ads. Instead, do your homework *before* contacting a credit counseling company. By the way, Fair Isaac officials say that entering a DMP does not hurt your credit score, despite what you may have heard.

Do check out any debt management firm by contacting the Better Business Bureau. Do call your state Attorney General's office to see if there are any complaints or ongoing investigations against the company. Do ask about the company's standing with the local Chamber of Commerce. If you feel comfortable with what you learn, then go ahead and contact the company. Do avoid agencies with large fees; some are has high as 10% of your monthly payment. Do ask about all your alternatives. Do inquire about the agency's full range of services. Do insist that everything be spelled out in black and white. And if you ever feel cheated, do report any abuse to the Federal Trade Commission.

I'm often asked for recommendations from consumers who want reputable credit counseling help or assistance from legitimate debt management agencies. I can unequivocally recommend The National Foundation for Debt Management, a highly professional, fair, and reputable non-profit agency that offers budgeting advice, credit counseling and debt management services throughout the United States. I have visited NFDM's headquarters in Florida to personally meet with their management team and counseling staff, assess their operations, and review their financial literacy initiatives. I came away extremely impressed. And this was *after* I'd done my own homework on the organization, including confirming their positive rating with the Better Business Bureau and verifying that NFDM is a HUD-certified credit counselor. So based on all my research, I can say with confidence that NFDM is a top-notch resource if you face challenges with budgeting, credit or debt.

Some other well-known debt-counseling organizations are the National Foundation for Credit Counseling (NFCC), parent company of Consumer Credit Counseling Services (CCCS) of America, and GetOutOfDebt.org. CCCS is the oldest credit counseling service in the U.S. Every year, NFCC agencies counsel more than one million clients through nearly 1,000 locations across the United States and Puerto Rico. GetOutOfDebt.org is run by veteran credit expert Steve Rhode, who provides credit-related help, debt management information and educational services to consumers. The addresses, telephone numbers, and Internet websites for NFDM, NFCC and GetOutOfDebt.org are listed at the end of this book in **Appendix A**.

Day 27: Evaluate your existing insurance coverage

Make sure you have adequate protection for your home and vehicle, as well as life and disability insurance. This step will strengthen your finances and protect you and your family. The American Council of Life Insurers suggests life insurance coverage of five to 10 times your annual salary. Visit www.insure.com to get rates on term or whole life insurance. Remember that good credit can translate into lower insurance premiums, as well.

Get a Clue – Your CLUE Insurance Report

In addition to checking your credit files and credit scores, you should also get your CLUE reports (short for "Comprehensive Loss Underwriting Exchange), which are files containing your auto and homeowner's insurance claim history. Most insurers use a company called LexisNexis Risk Solutions (formerly ChoicePoint) to get your insurance history – so you should know that too, because the information contained in the report is used—in addition to your FICO score—to determine your premiums.

LexisNexis' consumer website can be found at https://www.personalreports.lexisnexis.com. At this website, you'll be able to get your CLUE reports free of charge; you can also call 1-866-312-8076 for the reports. Under the FACT ACT, your CLUE reports are free once every 12 months. Check the reports to make sure everything is accurate. You don't want misinformation in these files to force you to pay higher insurance premiums. Just be aware, though, that since the average homeowner files a claim just once every 10 years, and the LexisNexis data is only kept for seven years, most people have a clean or non-existent CLUE report.

Who Needs Life Insurance, Anyway?

Don't operate under the misconception that life insurance is only for people who work full-time. Sophia Lezin was once surfing the Internet when a pop-up advertisement solicited her to buy life insurance. Not one to normally respond to such offers, Lezin nevertheless did answer the ad – and now she's glad she did.

A mother of two boys, Lezin's youngest son, Luke, was born on Thanksgiving Day. She later hopped onto a website and purchased a $500,000 life-insurance policy to protect her family in the event of her death.

"I just felt a big sense of relief," Lezin said.

In a lot of ways, Lezin, who lived in Montclair, NJ at the time, is the exception to the rule. Experts estimate that only a tiny fraction of the nation's stay-at- home parents buy life insurance – even though it could prove just as valuable to their families as it is to the families of working parents. Moreover, most Americans – in or out of the workforce – are believed to be significantly under-insured.

While the average U.S. household has an income of about $55,000, the typical American household has life insurance of only about $115,000, industry statistics show.

So how much protection do you need if you're not bringing home cash income? Statistics – and thus, the advice in this regard – vary widely. Jeremy White, a CPA in Paducah, KY, did some research to figure out the value of the services provided by a stay-at-home parent. His conclusion: the typical at-home mom renders about $60,000 in annual services.

Meanwhile, financial planner Ric Edelman, who runs Edelman Financial Services in Fairfax, VA, believes an at-home mother's services are worth far more. According to Edelman, the 17 occupational duties a mother carries out – everything from childrearing to managing household finances to resolving family emotional problems – are more adequately valued at $508,700 in wages. (Edelman arrived at that figure by adding up the median annual salaries of the 17 occupations).

Experts do generally agree, however, that for most stay-at-home moms and dads, term life insurance is your best option. Compared with permanent life insurance, term life insurance is the most affordable and often most appropriate. It protects you for a specific time frame, such as a 10- or 20- year period, and the premiums are fixed.

If you're a stay-at-home parent, you should know that some companies cap the amount of insurance they sell to you at $250,000. In Lezin-Jones' case, she was able to purchase twice that amount, for around $400 a year. She got the increased protection after explaining to her insurer that she planned to re-enter the workforce in the next few years.

To learn more about life insurance, and to comparison shop for the best prices, check out either of the following websites:

www.insure.com

www.insurance.com

Financial experts at www.insure.com also offer a comprehensive way to evaluate your specific life insurance needs. The guidelines they suggest are based on a variety of factors, including your short-term needs (for things like outstanding debts and emergency expenses); your long-term needs (for expenses such as mortgage payments); education (to cover your dependents' college tuition); your family's maintenance needs (to pay for child care, food, clothing, utility bills, insurance and transportation) and your current assets (including existing savings, stocks, bonds, mutual funds and other life insurance).

Five Types of Insurance That You Don't Need

Although I advocate buying insurance as a way to protect your family's interest, I also think there are some forms of insurance that are largely unnecessary. They are:

1. **Hospital indemnity Insurance**

   A policy can cost a few hundred dollars per year, but it only provides you roughly $100 per day of cash coverage to pay for expenses if you're hospitalized. That's not a lot, when you consider that the average hospital stay costs about $1,200 a day.

2. **Extended warranty/extended contract insurance**

   This policy is offered anytime you buy electronics or big-ticket items like DVD players or refrigerators. Usually the cost is very high and not worth it. Plus, when you buy on credit, the credit card company often extends the manufacturer's warranty.

3. **"Specific-health" insurance policies**

   This insurance protects you in the event you get cancer, suffer a stroke, or develop some specific disease. The problem is that this type of insurance is too narrow in terms of the coverage it provides, and these policies often have many exclusions.

4. **Life insurance for children**

   Life insurance is meant to replace the income of the person who dies, to take care of that person's heirs. Unless your kid makes a ton of money, or is in some way earning the family's primary income, life insurance for children is a total waste of money.

5. **Flight insurance**

It only pays off if you die or get badly injured in a plane crash. And statistically the chances of that happening are extremely small. Don't confuse this coverage, though, with trip interruption or travel cancellation insurance, which can actually come in handy once in a while.

Day 28: Draw up a will.

Wills aren't just for rich people. A last will and testament is a must for anyone with young children. You also need a will if you have anything at all of value – even sentimental value, like your wedding ring, a favorite coat or a treasured book collection. In the event of your death, a will tells the state (and your family) who should take care of your children, and who should get what, in terms of your assets. Wills can also help reduce family squabbling and the drama of grieving relatives arguing over how to divide your things. If you don't have the money to pay an attorney to create a will, for now use software programs or buy the ready-made wills found in office supply stores such as Staples, OfficeMax and Office Depot.

For online forms or step-by-step software to make a will, go to:

www.nolo.com (800-728-3555)
www.legalzoom.com (800-773-0888)
www.uslegalwills.com (888-660-WILL)

7 out of 10 adults in the U.S. don't have a will. That's a big financial mistake. If you die without a will, the courts in your state decide what happens with your assets – however large or small they may be. The courts can also determine who should take custody of any minor children you have. And the courts' decisions may be contrary to your wishes. Creating a will doesn't have to break your budget. An attorney can help you draw up a basic will for as little as $250 to $500. The price depends on where you live and the complexity of your situation. A cheaper option is to create a will online. At legalzoom.com, you can create a standard will and testament for $69. Also, USLegalWills.com offers basic wills online for just

$34.95. If you do use an Internet company, after you create your will, be sure to get it notarized and signed by at least two witnesses.

Don't procrastinate! Draw up a will at once. Save money, if you must, by creating the will yourself with a store-bought form. But I still recommend having an attorney give it a final look to make sure it conforms to your state law. Also, remember to have two witnesses sign your will, and get it notarized by a notary public who can put a seal on the will. To get motivated about making your will, think about your loved ones and fill out the form on the next page. You can also get this at AskTheMoneyCoach.com. Go to the Downloads section of the "Free Info" area, and then click on the proper PDF.

Get the Will to Draw Up a Will

I need an updated will because I would like to give my _____
(insert item) to _____ in the event of my death.
               (insert friend or relative's name)

I would also like to leave my _____ to _____
                      (insert item)   (insert name)

I need a will because I have a minor child (or children) named

_____

                    (insert name(s) here)

And to be a responsible parent, I want to appoint a guardian to ensure
his/ her (or their) well-being in my absence.

I need a will because upon my death, I wouldn't want to burden
_____ my _____
    (insert name)   (insert relationship, i.e. sister, husband, etc.)
with decisions that I should have made while I was alive.

Week 5 Overview

This week, you will:

√ Open a "hands-off" account and set up an automatic savings plan

√ Prepare yourself to become a positive financial role model

√ Address any other special circumstances in your life concerning money or credit

Day 29: Open a "hands off" account and set up an automatic savings plan

Go open a savings account at a credit union without a lot of branches, a bank that's far away from your home and job, or a small financial institution that doesn't offer ATM cards. Your goal is to have a "hands off" account where it's somewhat difficult or inconvenient to access your money. This way, you won't constantly withdraw it. Also, have your employer set up automatic payroll deductions from your paycheck to go into that "hands off" account. Even if it's just a small amount, start your automatic savings plan immediately. If you don't get your hands on the money, you won't miss it as much! The earlier you start saving and investing, the better. If you save $150 a month, then invest it and earn 10% annually, here's how it will grow:

	Actual $ Saved	**Your $ w/interest at each year-end**
Year 1	$1,800	$1,980
Year 2	$3,600	$3,967
Year 3	$5,400	$6,267
Year 4	$7,200	$8,808
Year 5	$9,000	$11,615
Year 10	$18,000	$30,726
Year 20	$36,000	$113,905
Year 30	**$54,000**	**$339,073**

See the power of compounded interest?

Note: Compounded interest can work for or against you. When you have credit card bills, you pay lots of compounded interest instead of *collecting* it!

Day 30: Prepare to become a positive financial role model

If you're like most adults, you probably want your children, or any youngsters around you, to develop good financial habits. But if you're like the typical American, you may also struggle when it comes to being a good financial role model for our youth. A study by Northwestern Mutual revealed that 71% of parents feel that children should begin learning about money no later than the 1st grade.

Yet, nearly half of parents say they do not set a good example when it comes to handling money, and that they are not capable of properly teaching their children to manage money. To boost your financial literacy, enroll in an adult education class on personal finances. To educate yourself about investing, join the National Association of Online Investors (www.naoi.org), which has great online study courses. For resources, fun games, tips and ideas for teaching youngsters about money, log onto www.nefe.org or call the National Endowment for Financial Education at 303-741-6333.

A Northwestern Mutual survey also found that less than 40% of parents talked about credit cards, loans and debt, and their own family finances with their kids. Fewer than one in four parents (23%) talked to their children about how to invest.

When asked why each topic was not raised for family discussion, most responded, *"Children have no business knowing this."* Others said they *"didn't think of it"* or that they considered their children too young to broach these issues.

But researchers also suggest another theory.

"It is almost certainly lack of confidence with their own financial management skills that keeps parents from discussing some of the more complex, and key, money issues with their children," says

Mark Schug, professor and Director of the University of Wisconsin-Milwaukee Center for Economic Education.

If you are a parent or educator who would like more information and free materials on personal finance education, check out www.themint.org. That website, jointly run by Northwestern Mutual and the National Council on Economic Education (www.ncee.net), offers practical tips, lesson plans, newsletters and interactive challenges to help teach kids of all ages about money.

Most experts caution that you can't rely on the school system to teach your kids about money and finance.

"The lack of financial literacy in this country is really a shame," says Bob Barry, former chairman of the Financial Planning Association. "Unfortunately, most schools are doing a terrible job of teaching the youth the basics about finance and investing."

Financial professionals nationwide echo Barry's sentiments.

For example, experts at the Greenwood Village, Colorado-based National Endowment for Financial Education sometimes find it difficult to get school districts throughout the country to allow NEFE representatives to come into their schools and provide proper financial training and education. NEFE (www.NEFE.org) has a cadre of capable and energetic volunteers on hand, and it offers financial education free of charge. Still, the organization frequently hears from administrators "we already teach that." A review of the existing curricula, though, most often reveals a shell of a program or very basic things, like how to open a bank account.

By contrast, NEFE teaches Americans – mainly high school students – practical money management skills, such as setting financial goals, developing a budget and understanding the pros and cons of using credit. The organization also introduces teens to more sophisticated subjects, including insurance, investments, taxes, and retirement planning. While NEFE offers a fine program, financial literacy isn't just for the youth. Most adults sailed through high school and even college without knowing a stock from a bond. As a result, many of us could also benefit from getting a solid financial education.

Teaching Kids about Choices with Money

There are a few other companies and initiatives that I consider enormously helpful for any parent, educator or adult who wants to teach kids about money – or even improve their own financial knowledge. One of them is the JumpStart Coalition for Personal Financial Literacy, which has a fabulous website: www.jumpstart. org, with great educational resources for youth of all ages (kindergarten through 12th grades).

Hands on Banking is another wonderful program by Wells Fargo that teaches money skills for four age groups, ranging from fourth graders to adults. The curriculum is fun to use, free of charge, and available in both English and Spanish. A bonus element of this curriculum is that anyone can use it, because it's designed for self-paced, individual learning, as well as for classroom and community groups. Get more info at www.handsonbanking.com.

Day 31: Address any other money woes, credit issues, or special financial circumstances

Throughout *Zero Debt*, I've attempted to cover a host of common situations that consumers with credit or money management issues face. But there are a host of other economic dilemmas, and you may still need to address some of these special situations to achieve financial freedom. Read on to find out if any of these scenarios apply to you. Or, if the information you learn in the following pages could help someone you know, be sure to share it with him or her.

Bankruptcy: Your Last-Ditch Option

The number of debt-laden consumers seeking bankruptcy protection from their creditors has reached unprecedented levels. In 2005, a record 2.1 million households declared bankruptcy. While that number may have dwindled to just over 1 million in 2015, Americans are still turning towards bankruptcy as a last resort from their financial woes.

If you're one of the many consumers filing for bankruptcy – or considering it – please think long and hard before you take this extremely drastic step. My experience in talking to consumers has been that most attorneys specializing in this area are quick to advise people to file for bankruptcy. On the other side, many credit counselors may tell you to never, ever file for bankruptcy. Obviously, there's no one-size-fits-all solution here. But I believe that even if you're drowning in debt, bankruptcy should be a last resort – contemplated only after you've truly exhausted all other possibilities. You should also know a few basic facts before you entertain the prospect of a bankruptcy. For starters, filing for bankruptcy isn't free – or even cheap. Expect to pay $500 to $1,000 or more in court filing fees and attorneys costs, depending on where you live and the complexity of your situation. Bankruptcy also doesn't get rid of all types of debt. For instance, spousal and child support obligations are not dischargeable in bankruptcy; and in most cases, neither are student loans and tax debts.

In *Everyone's Money Book on Credit*, author and personal finance expert Jordan Goodman notes that declaring bankruptcy is no panacea, because a bankruptcy filing remains on your credit for seven to 10 years and hampers your ability to secure future credit.

"Potential employers and landlords may also learn that you declared bankruptcy," Goodman says. "Therefore, bankruptcy is not exactly the fresh start that many lawyers advertise."

Another consideration: bankruptcy may really haunt you much longer than the decade that it is listed on your credit report. How so? Some job or credit applications ask you: Have you ever filed for bankruptcy? Even if your bankruptcy was 15 years ago, you're legally required to say "Yes." If you lie, you've just committed a crime.

The Consumer Education Center of the American Bankruptcy Institute, a non-partisan agency, says you may want to consider bankruptcy in the following situations:

- Your wages have been garnished or your bank account has been attached
- Most of your debts are unsecured, like credit card bills, hospital or doctor's bills, etc.
- Your total debt, not including your a car or house loan, is more than you could pay, even over five or more years
- Collection agencies are calling you at home and/or at work

- Your payments are more than 30 days behind on more than one bill
- There are lawsuits pending against you
- You have high medical bills not covered by insurance
- You owe income taxes that you are unable to currently pay
- You have few assets
- You have little or no savings
- You have had property repossessed (such as a vehicle)

I think these are good guidelines. But don't feel compelled to rush over to bankruptcy court just because you fit one of these criteria. Certainly, though, if you find yourself saying *"Yes, that's my situation"* to several of these areas, then it's time to at least weigh your options.

Bankruptcy Reform – What You Must Know

There are two main types of bankruptcy plans for consumers in the U.S. The first is a Chapter 7 filing, known as "liquidation," which is where you get to write off debts that you can't pay. The second form of bankruptcy for individuals is a Chapter 13 filing, which is called a "wage-earner repayment plan." Under Chapter 13, you pay back, some, but not all, of your debts, based on what you can afford.

In October 2005, a sweeping overhaul to the bankruptcy system in America occurred. Congress passed the Bankruptcy Abuse Prevention and Consumer Protection Act, in a purported effort to stop people from walking away from their debts when they had the ability to repay. The bottom line is that you can't simply wipe out your debts in bankruptcy court the way you once could. To be eligible for a Chapter 7 filing, not only do you have to go through credit counseling within 180 days of your filing, you must also show that you don't have the ability to pay back your creditors.

You must submit a form showing your monthly income and expenses. Under the new law, if you want to file for Chapter 7 bankruptcy protection, you must now pass an income test and a "means" test. The income test compares your income to the median income in your state, based on the number of people in your household. If your income exceeds your state median income, the bankruptcy trustee or any creditor can bring a motion to dismiss your bankruptcy filing on the grounds that is an "abuse" of the bankruptcy system. The "means" test involved in a Chapter 7 filing examines whether or not you can afford to pay a certain amount (at least $124.58 a month) to your creditors over the course of five years (a total of $7,474.58). If you are deemed capable of repaying this amount, you'll be shifted from Chapter 7 into Chapter 13 for five year's repayment.

Restoring Your Credit after Bankruptcy

If you've been through a bankruptcy, you probably feel like you've been through the ringer, personally, emotionally and financially. But don't despair. You can regain your financial footing little by little. Here are three ways to re-build your credit after bankruptcy.

1. **Avoid sub-prime credit cards**

   These cards have high interest rates and ridiculously high fees. It's not uncommon to find sub-prime cards, at 20% interest, that give you a $500 credit limit, but then impose $200 or more in miscellaneous fees. So right off the bat, you're in debt, and the credit limit you have is far lower than you expected.

2. **Do business with a Credit Union**

   Credit unions' mission is to serve their client's best interests. They're not out to gouge you and make a king's ransom on your economic misfortune or your financial naivety. In fact, they're very good at providing financial literacy and education, if necessary. So if you need a loan or credit card after a bankruptcy, try a credit union. Find one via the Credit Union National Association at www.cuna.org.

3. **Get a Secured Credit Card**

   Don't stress yourself out if you can't get a regular credit card after your bankruptcy has been discharged. Instead, start small. Get a secured card, where you have to put up cash into an account. The amount you put up, let's say it's $500, is typically your credit limit. Just pay your bills on time every month and you will slowly but surely establish a track record of someone who is credit-worthy. Soon you'll find that other, better credit offers come your way.

Delinquent Taxes: What to Do about Them

If you owe back taxes to the government, a little-known measure of recourse is to propose an "Offer in Compromise" to settle your delinquent tax bill. Most taxing authorities will accept a lump sum or a payment plan for less than the amount you owe, to settle old taxes. Some of the entities that will consider an "Offer in Compromise" are the Internal Revenue Service, the Franchise Tax Board, and the State Board of Equalization. They'll even be willing to negotiate to lower any late fees and interest charges that have accumulated, along with self-employment or Medicare taxes due.

If you've lost your job, retired, got sick, had a business that went bust, or have filed bankruptcy, you have pretty good odds of getting a tax authority to accept your "Offer in Compromise" – or at least be amenable to working out some mutually acceptable deal with you. The reason is that the Offer in Compromise program was designed to collect back taxes that the government might otherwise never collect. In some cases, people who owe tax debts have been able to pay anywhere from 10 cents to 50 cents on the dollar when they work out an "Offer in Compromise" as a settlement.

If you'd like to learn more about this topic, read up on the subject at www.nolo.com or by checking out the numerous articles I've written about this area. You can find my articles on my blog, AskTheMoneyCoach.com.

Helping Aging Parents with Their Finances

If you have elderly parents, it should come as no surprise that the older Mom and Dad get, the more vulnerable they are to a host of medical and financial challenges.

CPAs recommend that you discuss medical and financial issues with your aging parents periodically. Changes in their health or financial situation, as well as ever-changing tax laws, could affect how they plan for and protect their future.

Unfortunately, too many of us shy away from talking to our parents about money matters – even when an older parent's deteriorating health starts to greatly impact his or her financial well-being.

If you've ever found it difficult to talk to your parents about their finances, follow these tips to open the lines of communication, and to safeguard your parents' financial health.

- **Acknowledge Your Parents' Perspective – And Your Own**
  Susan Richards, a certified financial planner in Chicago and the author of *Protect Your Parents and Their Financial Health ... Talk With Them Before It's Too Late* believes it's natural to feel squeamish inquiring about how well (or how poorly) a parent is doing financially. The reason? Having that conversation "changes the dynamic of the parent-child relationship" she says. That feels like a role reversal, in which you are now the caretaker, and that's likely to be unfamiliar and uncomfortable territory.

  Additionally, you may feel ill equipped to manage your own finances, let alone give your parents guidance about how to manage theirs. If this is the case, seek professional help from a qualified financial advisor.

- **Realize That Helping Your Parents is a Process, Not an Event**
  Ask your parents what small steps you can take to continually aid them. Maybe you can pay their bills online, see that their bank accounts are properly credited for deposits, or do their weekly shopping. Engage them in the process, though, by inquiring directly about exactly where they need assistance in handling their day- to-day finances.

  Tip: If your parents receive a Social Security check each month, you should visit a nearby Social Security Administration office and ask to be made a representative payee. The SSA will conduct an investigation and, if you check out, the agency will appoint you to act on your parents' behalf. You can then use those funds to set up automatic monthly payments for your parents' recurring bills.

- **Know Where Important Records Are Located**

  Ask your parents to prepare a list of their assets, liabilities and other pertinent financial information. As gently as possible, make it clear that you need to know where relevant documents are – such as a will, medical cards or insurance policies – in case something happens to them. A great book to help you is *Checklist for My Family: A Guide to My History, Financial Plans, and Final Wishes.* Sally Hurme, an elder advocate, former attorney and ex staffer at AARP, wrote it.

- **Consider Drawing Up Appropriate Legal Documents**

  But don't just give your parents a piece of paper (or even worse, mounds of paperwork) to fill out. That will just overwhelm them. Instead, have a conversation about what they would like to do with their assets, how they would like their affairs to be handled in the event of their incapacitation, and what they would prefer to happen upon their death.

  The California Society of Certified Public Accountants recommends that adult parents weigh a number of options, including establishing durable powers of attorney, trusts, living wills and joint bank accounts. All these documents require your parents' signature while they are still capable of conveying those powers to you or someone else. Many legal experts favor a durable power of attorney. That allows a parent to give another person, usually a spouse or a child, permission to handle their financial affairs if the individual in question suffers an illness such as a stroke or develops a condition like Alzheimer's. An ordinary power of attorney is not valid once a person becomes incapacitated.

- **Take advantage of appropriate resources and government agencies**

  Contact the Social Security Administration for a report on your parents' earnings history, along with estimates of their retirement, disability and death benefits, if they don't have it already. Call 1- 800-772-1213 or visit the website www.ssa.gov. The form you'll need is called a <u>Request for Earnings and Benefit Estimate Statement</u>.

  Finally, The Eldercare Locator, (800) 677-1116, is a nationwide, directory assistance service that helps you find an array of services of the elderly – everything from home care to transportation to legal and social services. Visit the website at www.eldercare.gov. The Eldercare Locator is a public service of the Administration on Aging, (www.aoa.gov) and the U.S. Department of Health and Human Services.

Student Loans: The Other Big Debt Crisis in America

If you have credit card debt, you already know how stressful it can be to manage those payments. But if you're among the millions of people out there who are also burdened by student loan debt, then you're dealing with a one-two financial punch that can knock you out if you're not careful. Americans are coming out of school more indebted than ever. The typical graduate of the Class of 2016 left college with roughly $37,000 in student loans, according to the College Board. If you went to graduate school, tack another $40,000 in college debt on that figure. And for those of you who've attended medical school or law school, you know it's not uncommon to wind up with $100,000 or more in school-related debt.

The student loan crisis is such an important subject that I've written an entire book about it. It's a sequel to *Zero Debt*, and it's called *Zero Debt for College Grads: From Student Loans to Financial Freedom*. If you, your children, or anyone you know has student loans, I strongly urge you to get this book immediately. In the meantime, here are some tips for current students, college graduates and parents who all grapple with student loan debt.

Golden Rules for Student Borrowers

Are you worried about the skyrocketing costs of college and financing your education with student loans? If so, you're not alone. About 70% of college graduates in America leave school with student-loan debt and chances are you're one of them, or you soon will be. Fortunately, if you're a student, there are some things you can do to help yourself out of a student loan dilemma, as well as assist future college graduates who, if things remain the same, will have it even worse than you do.

Here are seven golden rules for student borrowers.

Rule #1: Don't over-estimate your starting income

One of the biggest wake-up calls for students and recent college graduates is once you get out of school, *Bam!* You're hit with a host of costs – not to mention student loans – but your salary might be far below what you expected. What's the solution? Be realistic about your earnings outlook. Don't assume you're going to pull down a six-figure income as soon as you get that degree. Even if you do work in a field where six-figure salaries are the norm, chances are you have to work yourself up to that level. It won't happen automatically. Take a look, for example, at the most lucrative degrees for college graduates who recently left school. The numbers are solid, but they're not blockbuster figures, especially if you've got $30,000 or more worth of college debt with which to contend.

Most Lucrative Degrees for College Grads

Rank	Major	Average starting salary
1	Engineering	$62,998
2	Computer Science	$61,287
3	Math and Science	$56,171
4	Business	$51,508
5	Agriculture/Natural Resources	$51,220
6	Healthcare	$50,839
7	Communications	$49,395
8	Social Sciences	$49,047
9	Humanities	$49,042

[Source: National Association of Colleges and Employers; 2015 data]

By the way, at the bottom of the rung were Liberal Arts majors, like those with degrees in History or English. Their starting salaries were in the $36,000 range. Meanwhile, Marketing majors scored salaries that came in at the $42,000 level. So take your starting salary into consideration when you accept student loans.

Rule #2: Pick Your Poison

If you know your financial aid package won't cover all your school costs and living expenses, be smart about what sources of funding you select to make up the difference. Don't rely on high-interest- rate credit cards, and always – without exception

– get federal loans first, before you turn to the private loan market to finance college. Be cautious about taking out private loans because, unlike federal loans, they have variable interest rates, are usually more expensive, contain no loan forgiveness or cancellation features, and are unsubsidized (this means that while you're in school, you have to pay the interest on your loans immediately. With subsidized federal loans, the government pays the interest on your debt while you're enrolled at least half-time).

Whether you choose a federal or private loan, make sure you shop around and get the best possible deal from your lender. Seek out lenders that offer few or no loan origination fees, lower interest rates for automatic deductions, or better rates for making a specific number of payments on time. Many lenders will cut your interest rate after you've made a set number of timely payments. Depending on the lender, it's usually 12, 24 or 48 payments. The bottom line is: be a smart consumer when you have to borrow money for college.

Rule #3: Be Wise about Consolidating

Make sure you don't consolidate in ways that could hurt you in the long run. For instance, don't consolidate private and federal loans together. If you consolidate Perkins loans, they have better forgiveness benefits for people who go into teaching, and you can lose those benefits if you consolidate them.

Rule #4: Demand Accountability and Rational Behavior from Colleges and Universities

Recently, the *New York Times* reported on a trend about how many schools were artificially raising the price of tuition to help their college rankings and to appear more attractive to students and families. The thinking among these schools was: if we cost more, prospective students and their families will automatically assume we're "better" schools. Unfortunately, this crazy logic has worked. But one of the reasons colleges get away with charging sky-high tuition rates is that they know many parents will do whatever it takes, and make sacrifices – even unwise ones – just to help their children obtain a college degree. Don't fall for these kinds of tactics. Ask your school officials if what they charge really covers the cost of education or if that money's going elsewhere.

Rule #5: Voice Your Concerns Publicly
Make your thoughts about the student loan crisis known to others, especially your local representatives and members of Congress. Lawmakers are listening and know that student loans are a huge problem. That's why they voted in 2007 to slash interest rates on federal Stafford loans from 6.8% to 3.4% over the course of five years. This has saved borrowers a ton of money. As of this writing, Stafford loans taken out in 2016-2017, carry a 3.76% rate. Keep the focus on this issue. Let lawmakers know what it's like to be forced to take on student loans just to have a shot at a better quality of life. Urge politicians to increase grants to students, not loans. You can get in touch with your elected officials at both the state and the federal level. To find out the names of your elected officials, visit http://www.congress.org.

Rule #6: Form or Join Student Advocacy Groups
Get help from initiatives and organizations like the Project on Student Debt (http:// www.projectonstudentdebt.org), the United States Student Association (http://www.usstudents.org), an

advocacy group for college students, as well as the local student Public Interest Research Group (http:// www.uspirg.org) in your area. These can all be powerful resources through which you can mobilize and join the fight against enormous student loan debt.

Rule #7: Start Your Own Business – or at Least Get a Job!

Let's face it: most students have to work to help foot their college bills. But why work for someone else when you can be your own boss, and make lots of money in the process? A good book on this topic is *Campus CEO* by Randal Pinkett, which describes how today's college students don't have to wait to have a career. You can launch a business now – even while you're in school – helping you earn money and avoid educational debt. If entrepreneurship is out of the question, at least consider a part-time job to reduce your need for college loans.

By decreasing your dependency on loans, and being smart about managing the educational debt you may already have, you'll start off your post-college life on solid financial ground. By the way, I know about this topic from first-hand experience. After undergraduate and graduate school, I had nearly $40,000 in student loans. Fortunately, I've managed to pay them off and not have student loans wreak havoc on my finances. If you'd like more advice on this topic, check out my free advice at AskTheMoneyCoach.com or pick up a copy of my book *Zero Debt for College Grads*. It contains everything that students, graduates and parents need to know about paying off student loans, and juggling day-to-day bills.

7 Financial Tips for Parents Regarding College Loans

For those of you who are parents, it's understandable that you want to help your child avoid the plague of student loan debt, but there's a right way to go about doing it and a wrong way. The wrong way is to completely sacrifice your financial future, forgoing retirement savings and just "hoping for the best" when you're in your Golden Years. The right way is to approach college with some smart financial planning. Take these tips to reduce the student loan burden that you – and your kid – will face later in life.

Tip #1: Save for College as Early as Possible

You already know how expensive college is right now. But have you factored in college inflation for the future? Already the annual price tag for some public schools exceeds $30,000 a year, and an incredible $60,000 or more for many private colleges, including Ivy League schools. Unfortunately, 31% of parents who plan to help pay for college haven't started saving yet. Start socking away as much as you can now to decrease the need for loans in the future.

Tip #2: Open a 529 Plan

A 529 College Savings Plan is the best thing going when it comes to saving for your child's college education. Available in every state in the country, a 529 Plan is portable and can be used at any qualifying institution of higher learning in America. It's a great way to sock away tens of thousands of dollars annually for higher educational expenses, because money in a 529 Plan grows tax-free if it's used for college costs. Many states even give you a tax deduction for contributing to a 529. Best of all: these plans are maintained in your (or the donor's) name, so they don't reduce your child's chances for receiving financial aid. For more info on 529 Plans, visit http://www.savingforcollege.com.

Tip #3: Plan for Some Aid

Unless you can truly afford it without changing your whole lifestyle, strike a balance between trying to fund your kids' college account, and planning to get some need-based aid. There's no rule that says you have to foot your son or daughter's entire college tuition bills, plus pay for all his or her living expenses and other needs.

Apply for aid, but don't over-estimate how much your child will get. Although 72% of parents think their kids could get merit aid, the reality is that only 28% of students currently do. Your child's financial aid package will be based on your income and assets, the cost of the school, and whether you have other children in college. Take your entire situation into account when you're thinking about aid. Do you have more kids or other family members who'll need money for school or other reasons? Also be mindful of your own income picture – not to mention rising healthcare costs, current bills, and the need to save for your own retirement.

Tip #4: Impose a Spending Cap

It's very easy to lose track of money spent on college. You can write a check here or there for living expenses, allow your child to take money out of your account, pay his or her credit card, and send in tuition payments to school – and before you know it you've spent many thousands of dollars. There is a better strategy.

Sit down and talk with your son or daughter and set a budget. Explain what is financially feasible and possible for you to do – and what isn't. If all you can afford to give (or take out in loans) is, say $5,000 or $10,000 a year, then put that number on the table as your limit, then stick to it. For some advice on how much debt you can realistically manage, go to a financial planner who specializes in college financing. You can get a referral from the National Institute of Certified College Planners (NICCP) at http://www.niccp.com. Alternatively, any number of college financing calculators that are available online, such as the one at FinAid (http://www.finaid.org/ calculators).

Tip #5: Don't Skip Your Retirement Savings

Experts from the National Institute of Certified College Planners agree with me that you shouldn't sacrifice your retirement to pay for or borrow money for your child's education. Think about it this way: Little Johnny might be able to borrow for college, but who's going to loan you money for your retirement? I know this may seem like tough love, but it's foolish to put yourself in the hole financially in ways that make it almost impossible for you to recover. Unfortunately, many parents do exactly that. I know it's out of love for your kids. I would do most anything for my kids too. But some of the things we do as parents really don't serve our children's best interest, or our own long-term well-being.

Check out these findings from various surveys, which polled parents about their children in college:

- 66% of parents say they will have to delay retirement because they've helped put their kids through college [Source: Alliance Bernstein Investments]

- 17% are working or plan to work second jobs to help pay for their children's college education [Source: Fidelity Investments]
- 32% of parents intend to take out a second mortgage to pay for tuition [Source: Rasmussen Reports]
- Nearly 30% of parents have had an adult child return home after graduating from college [Source: Pew Research Center]

Again, it's no sin to help your child succeed – and education is one way to do so. It is a travesty, however, when you get sent to the poorhouse in the process.

Tip #6: Allow Your Child to Borrow First

This is a more cost-effective way to take on college debt, since federal Stafford Loans stand at a maximum interest rate of 3.76% for undergraduate students, but PLUS loans (Parent Loans for University Students), which are made to parents, now carry a 6.31% interest rate.

Tip #7: Use College Saver Programs like Upromise.com and Littlegrad.com

When you enroll in these programs, a small portion of the money you spend on everyday things – like gas for your car, clothes purchases or entertainment – gets funneled into a savings account for your child. Heck, if you were going to spend the money anyway, you might as well get a little rebate for that spending, which can help pay down college expenses.

All parents understandably want a better life for their children, both in terms of their personal happiness and their financial security.

Following the steps I've outlined above will go a long way toward helping you and your kids become debt free.

Payday Loans: 'Credit' You Must Never Accept

I usually try to refrain from giving absolutes when dispensing personal finance wisdom. But this is an area where I want to be extremely clear: Never, ever, ever get a payday loan.

If you've taken a payday loan before, then you probably know that you're being charged loan-shark rates – worse than most loan sharks charge, as a matter of fact. But for those of you new to this world, here are the facts.

- Payday loans are short terms loans made by financial "institutions." These loans are designed to "tide people over" until they get their paycheck.
- Payday loans work like this: A customer needs money before he gets his paycheck next Friday. To make ends meet he goes to a payday lender who verifies that the individual has a legitimate job and a bank checking account. The customer gets a $300 "loan" – immediate cash in exchange for writing a postdated $300 check to the payday lender. This check is cashed once the individual's payday rolls around. But the payday lender doesn't actually give the consumer $300. Instead the customer will get $255; the other $45 is the fee or interest cost associated with taking this payday loan.
- On an annualized basis, payday loans like the previous example work out to be about 400% per year. Some have effective Annual Percentage Rates (APRs) of nearly 800%.

- The average person who takes out a payday loan gets one per month, or twelve per year.
- Regulators and consumer protection groups are all worried about how payday lenders operate, especially their aggressive collection practices (*see* **Day 9**). The Federal Trade Commission, Consumers Union and the Consumer Federation of America have all expressed concern about the payday loan industry.
- Cash-strapped consumers often "roll over" their payday loans multiple times, and wind up paying more than 1,000% in interest, according to a study by Georgetown University researchers.
- By partnering with certain financial institutions, and skirting various statutes, payday lenders are able to get around state "usury laws," legislation that prevents lending entities from charging sky-high interest rates.
- Despite their marketing efforts to make payday loans seem legitimate, several corporation heads of payday loans have recently (as of April 2016) been indicted or plead guilty to charges of racketeering, consumer fraud, money laundering, and a host of other unethical behaviors.

Bottom line: If you think regular old debt collectors bound by federal laws are hard to deal with, you definitely don't want to fool around with payday lenders and subject yourself to their shenanigans. Even if you're desperate for money to pay your debts, seek any other source of cash you can, such as a pay advance from your employer or a loan from a family member, rather than resort to payday loans.

If you've taken all the advice in Zero Debt, I know the last month has been fruitful and eye-opening. Keep track of your progress. And do let me know about your victories in conquering your debt and mastering your finances. To share your story or to ask me a money management or personal finance question, email me at info@AskTheMoneyCoach.com. Please also visit my website/blog to learn more smart ways to save, spend, or invest your money.

Here's wishing you *Zero Debt* status and financial freedom for a lifetime!

Lynnette Khalfani-Cox,
The Money Coach®

Appendix A: Credit Bureaus and Debt Management Firms

Equifax
P.O. Box 740241
Atlanta, GA 30374
www.equifax.com
800-685-1111

Experian
P.O. Box 2002
Allen, TX 75013
www.experian.com
888-397-3742

Trans Union
P.O. Box 2000
Chester, PA 19022
www.transunion.com
800-916-8800

Innovis
PO Box 219297
Houston, TX 77218-9297
www.innovis-cbc.com
800 540 2505

Debt Management and Credit Counseling Firms

National Foundation for Debt Management
14104 58th Street North;
Clearwater, FL 33760
www.nfdm.org; 866-409-6336

National Foundation for Credit Counseling (Parent org. of CCCS)
8605 Cameron Street, Suite M2;
Silver Spring, MD 29207
www.nfcc.org; 800-388-2227

GetOutOfDebt.org
Raleigh, North Carolina
GetOutOfDebt.org
888-919-3323

Appendix B: Sample Settlement Letter

Your Name
Your Address
Your City, State and Zip Code

Date

Name of Customer Service Rep
ABC Credit Card Company
ABC Credit Card Company Address
Their City, State and Zip Code

Via Certified Mail, Return Receipt Requested #_____

Re: Account# 444-333-222 with your company

Dear: _____

Per our telephone conversation of today, this letter is to confirm that I will send $250 to ABC Credit Card Co. as "Payment in Full" to settle the balance due on the above-referenced account.

Within seven days of receiving my $250 payment, ABC Credit Card Co. will delete from my credit report any negative references related to this account, and will update its records with the credit bureaus to reflect that my account has been "Paid in Full" or "Paid as Agreed."

Your signature below will verify your acceptance of these terms. After you return to me a signed copy of this agreement, I will immediately forward my $250 payment.

Thank you for your assistance with this matter.

Sincerely,   Date Agreement Signed: _____

_____   _____
Your Name   ABC Credit Representative

Appendix C: Sample Cease & Desist Letter

Your Name
Your Address
Your City, State and Zip Code

Date

Collection Agent Name
XYZ Collection Agency
XYZ Collection Agency Address
Their City, State and Zip Code

Via Certified Mail, Return Receipt Requested # _____

Re: Account# 123-456-789 with ABC Creditor

Dear _____ :

As I have told you in numerous telephone conversations, I am unable to pay the above referenced debt due to my job layoff.

I hereby assert my right, under Section 805-C of the Fair Debt Collection Practices Act, to request that you cease any further communication with me.

Sincerely,

Your Name

Appendix D: The 30-Day Zero Debt Challenge!

How many items can you do in 30 days?

Write down your start date, a Y for Yes, N for No, and the date you finish each task

Start Date:	Done?
Day — Action Item	Yes/No
1. Call 888-5-OPT-OUT	
2. Vow to 'stop digging'	
3. Put all debts in writing	
4. Order credit report	
5. Negotiate with creditors	
6. Switch credit cards	
7. Exceed min. payment	
8. Dispute credit errors	
9. Learn legal rights	
10. Stop harassment	
11. Thwart ID theft	
12. Set up filing system	
13. Face the truth	
14. Create SMART goals	
15. Analyze cash sources	
16. Scrutinize spending	

17. Set realistic budget	
18. Cut spending 10 ways	
19. Adopt 5 life changes	
20. Adjust W-4 withholdings	
21. Sell unwanted stuff	
22. Generate more income	
23. Get home equity line	
24. Refinance auto loan	
25. Pick debt payoff plan	
26. Consider debt mgmt.	
27. Evaluate insurance	
28. Draw up a will	
29. Open 'hands off' acct.	
30. Become a role model	

CONGRATULATIONS!

I want to hear all about your progress! After you finish "The 30-day Zero Debt Challenge," no matter how many items you've finished, e-mail me at info@askthemoneycoach.com to tell me how you did.

If you want to get an 8 ½ by 11-inch copy of "The 30-Day Zero Debt Challenge," please visit the "Free Info" section at AskTheMoneyCoach.com and follow the link to the proper PDF. Print out this free download, then put it up on your wall to remind yourself of the action steps that will get you on the road to financial freedom *in just 30 days!*

Appendix E: Consumer Resources

Websites

www.askthemoneycoach.com

www.bankrate.com

www.capitalone.com

www.consumer.gov/idtheft

www.handsonbanking.com

www.myfico.com

www.salliemae.com

www.themint.org

Books

Everyone's Money Book on Credit by Jordan Goodman

Zero Debt for College Grads by Lynnette Khalfani-Cox

Checklist for My Family by Sally Hurme

Weapons of Math Destruction by Cathy O'Neill

Index

Notes

Made in the USA
Middletown, DE
09 January 2018